PRAISE FOR *INEXP...*

"Chelsea has inspired us for years as a chil[...] gating her life with grace, love, and humili[...] [n]ow brings to paper her inspiring story giving insight into finding your worth and path in life with humor and love. You will be inspired by her words and moved by her heart. We are so grateful that now so many will be able to benefit from her journey, especially our little one."

—**Jesse Tyler Ferguson**, Emmy Award–nominated actor, and
Justin Mikita, Tony Award–winning producer

"I've have had the privilege of watching Chelsea grow from a thoughtful young woman into a dynamic advocate. In her book, she gives you a glimpse of her world and how growing up with two gay dads, not only molded who she was, but gave her a base of unconditional love to carry her through her life. Of course, in *Inexplicably Me* she has chosen to inspire and encourage everyone to find their worth and their purpose, doing this while using her own story, with touching vulnerability, to ignite each reader's sense of possibility."

—**Joe Solomonese**, CEO of the Democratic National Convention
2020, and former president of the Human Rights Campaign

"Having known the wonderful Chelsea and her dads since she was a toddler it comes as no surprise that she has written an incredible piece about growing up as the daughter of gay dads. Her new book tells of her journey and how that inspired her to seek out, give back, and pursue worthiness at every level. With her charming style, warm wit, and incredible openness she gives you the tools you need to navigate this world with a strong sense of worth, gratitude, and purpose. Chelsea is a gem and her new book is a gold mine!"

—**Ed Harris and Amy Madigan**, Academy Award–nominated actors

INEXPLICABLY
ME

INEXPLICABLY ME

A STORY OF LABELS, WORTHINESS, AND REFUSING TO BE BOXED IN

CHELSEA AUSTIN MONTGOMERY-DUBAN WÄCHTER

Health Communications, Inc.
Boca Raton, Florida

www.hcibooks.com

This book is memoir. It reflects the author's recollections of experiences over time. Some names and characteristics have been changed and some events have been compressed.

Library of Congress Cataloging-in-Publication Data
is available through the Library of Congress

© 2022 Chelsea Austin Montgomery-Duban Wächter

ISBN-13: 978-07573-2427-7 (Paperback)
ISBN-10: 07573-24274 (Paperback)
ISBN-13: 978-07573-2428-4 (ePub)
ISBN-10: 07573-24282 (ePub)

All rights reserved. Printed in the United States of America. No part of this publication may be reproduced, stored in a retrieval system, or transmitted in any form or by any means, electronic, mechanical, photocopying, recording, or otherwise, without the written permission of the publisher.

HCI, its logos, and marks are trademarks of Health Communications, Inc.

Publisher: Health Communications, Inc.
        1700 NW 2nd Avenue
        Boca Raton, FL 33432-1653

Cover and interior design by Larissa Hise Henoch
Formatting by Lawna Patterson Oldfield

For Dad, Daddy, and Domi,
because we never can put into words
just how much we love each other.

"We did not know what to make of her.
In our minds we tried to pin her to a cork board like a butterfly,
but the pin merely went through and away she flew."
—**Jerry Spinelli,** *Stargirl*

CONTENTS

PREFACE

I sat crying in my car this morning. They were happy tears, and this is definitely not out of the ordinary for me. I was thinking of how, if I could make one wish for all humans on this planet, I would wish that every single day we all woke up with the courage to define ourselves regardless of who the world tells us to be.

I will never deny that the blessings and privilege I have benefitted from have given me an advantage, a huge one. I have always felt I was loved and wanted immeasurably, and my parents have always reminded me of that. The world was always my oyster. And in this beautiful bubble, I grew up thinking all kids thought as I did, believing they could do anything they set their minds to. I thought their parents must have also told them that anything is possible.

If every little kid had an angel who would love them as much as my parents loved me, then every one of us would believe there is room for everyone on the planet to have it all. Maybe we would be less competitive and more loving with each other. I may not have known how to express it as a little tyke, but as I got older, I realized the necessity of spreading the gospel of tolerance, which I believe starts with self-acceptance. Even if your parents did not teach you to love yourself like mine did, you can come to know that the world's love is unlimited, not divisible like pieces of pie.

I have come to realize over my twenty-seven years on this planet that there is a common factor among people who are achieving their dreams. Those who are able to find their purpose with inner peace refuse to let the world define them. They refuse to believe that they should be labeled by how they were raised, or where they were born, or their gender identity, race, religion, socioeconomic status, level of ability, or sexual orientation. Those who have chosen to find joy have looked at their surroundings and decided those surroundings are not limitations, or definitions, but springboards. Those who believe they can, can check step one off their list.

Just remember this:

- We define our worth.
- We approve of ourselves.
- We choose what we identify as.
- We are allowed to start over any time.
- Don't look out, look in.
- Expect the best.
- Breathe when things get tough.
- Love immensely and deeply—yourself and others.
- Have a vast amount of gratitude.
- Trust yourself.
- Laugh at yourself.
- Love.
- Take some deep breaths.
- Believe in yourself.

Okay, enough of this for now. Let's get to how I came to be who I am.

CHAPTER 1

BEFORE I HAD ANY NAMES

"The two most important days in your life are the day
you are born, and the day you find out why."

—**Mark Twain**

T
he story of how I came to be lands me in an incredibly stable household as an only child with two adoring and doting fathers. My dads had been together for eleven years when they decided to have me, so they were already seasoned vets in the long-term relationship department. Like many romantic comedies, they met on a blind date. It is a long and complicated story in which my dad's old roommate, Phoebe, and my dad's brother compete for being the reason Dad and Daddy got together.

By the way, I still call my parents Dad and Daddy. Don't you still call your parents Mom and Dad? I thought so . . .

I do often find myself explaining to strangers that, yes, I know it is strange that at twenty-seven I call one of my fathers Daddy, but there are two dads involved here. I call one Dad and the other Daddy; those are their names and that is the way it will be until the end of time.

It does get exhausting sometimes.

But before I get ahead of myself, let me set the stage. The beaches of Malibu, California, are where my story begins. My hometown. No, I am not kidding, and yes, it is paradise. I am blessed and beyond grateful to have grown up there. I did not really realize the whole paradise aspect of it until I spent four years away in Pennsylvania shoveling snow until my hands felt like they were going to fall off.

I have to say Malibu is one of the weirdest places in the world. It is a large tourist trap created by a fascination with fame. People come to see celebrities, and most of the stars they want to see do not even live here anymore. It is a gorgeous place, but most of our beaches do not even have toilets or trash cans, and I am sorry but you can't tell me that you can sit on a beach all day without going number one or number two at some point.

The summer can become insufferable with the heat and the traffic, and all of the people who actually live in Malibu run to Los Angeles International Airport and fly to any location not on the coast of California. And to be honest, who cares where we go?

I lived in a bubble for most of my life. I was raised in a place where everyone thought being gay was cool. I was also incredibly special—I was the only kid I knew with two gay dads where the kid was not from another marriage or adopted. I was a true test-tube baby (cue gasps and villagers with their pitchforks). I was conceived on a glorious day at UCLA hospital way back in 1992. Dad even got to see me in a Petri dish of four cells, and I am pretty sure he looks at me now the same way he looked at the Petri dish on that day: full of hope, joy, and wonder. I kind of wish I had been there to see his face.

Let me take you back to the beginning, before there was a little Chelsea Austin Montgomery-Duban, although I would like to believe time stood still until I came along.

Eleven years into Dad and Daddy's relationship, they decided to have a kid and knew they could not just get pregnant by happenstance. (No real shocker there considering they are two dudes.) They had to make the conscious decision to raise a child together, which I think is pretty amazing. They did not just wake up one day and think, "Hey, we should have a kid." There is, of course, a good story attached.

They had seen three friends in one week on different occasions and all three of their friends, out of the blue, had told Dad and Daddy they would make great parents. Well, that was a weird coincidence. So, my fathers took the long drive from Los Angeles up to their haven in Anacortes, Washington, to think about their next adventure in life.

I am not exactly sure what was said on the trip up to the Puget Sound, but here is something interesting about Dad and Daddy. My dad was born to have children. He always wanted to have a child, and when he realized at a very young age that he was gay, he became depressed thinking he could not have kids and the "picket fence" life he dreamed of. He perhaps could not have imagined as a young little gay guy that society and science would eventually come such a long way that he could, in fact, have a child—even one he was biologically related to. When he grew up, he surrounded himself with other people's children and taught children's theater. He is all-around just one of those humans with, let's say, amazing paternal instincts.

Daddy could not have been more different. If there was a kid within one mile of wherever he was, he would pray not to have to deal with them. He did not know how to hold a baby and found no joy in watching children play. They were exhausting, they were messy, and most of all, they did not do what you wanted them to. So, I imagine the conversation about having a child was interesting. But somehow, on the very long car ride, Dad must have said something right to get Daddy thinking that he, too, could love being a parent.

They knew if they were going to have a kid they did not want to adopt if there was another option. Adoption is an incredible act of selflessness and generosity, but it was not the way they wanted to have a child. They wanted to try to keep it all in the family. So, they needed to figure out whose sperm they were going to use, and then find an egg donor and a surrogate. Both my parents have younger sisters, and it was pretty easy to choose who they were going to ask to donate eggs, given that Dad's born-again Christian sister would probably not be so hot on the idea of donating an egg for her very-much-gay big brother to have a child with his male partner. They asked Daddy's sister, Auntie, as I called her, and she agreed without a moment's thought. She was ten years Daddy's junior and revered him in a way I have never seen a person revere another human. She would have done anything for him, and this was just the sort of way she could give back to him in a way that made her glow.

It was then pretty obvious that Dad would be the sperm donor because, had they used Daddy's sperm, I would have been my own first cousin... yeah, figure that one out.

Then they needed a surrogate. Auntie was not the right fit because she had no children of her own yet and they thought giving away her firstborn might be too traumatic. They thought and thought about a possible option, but no one came to mind. They did not particularly feel like hiring someone to do the job, and in 1992 it seemed difficult to find a surrogate who would carry a child for two gay men. Dad and Daddy arrived at the oasis, aka Anacortes, and decided they would each take an hour in separate rooms to make a list of potential surrogates, either family members or *very* close friends. After an hour, my dads emerged, Daddy with no one on his list and Dad with one name: Sandy.

Dad's cousin Sandy was one of his favorite people growing up. They adored each other. Sandy is easygoing and, dare I say, a bit emotionless to the outside observer. She already had two kids of her own and, without giving away too much personal information about her, she needed a reason to get out of Oklahoma where she had been living. Dad and Daddy called her, and she said she needed some time to think about this massive decision. She was already forty-five, so it would not be an easy pregnancy from the get-go. While she thought about it, my parents could not sit still, so they decided to get some Mexican food to take their minds off things—as if guacamole and chips could really get your mind off thinking about having a child of your own. When they got back from dinner, they immediately ran to the phone. The red light indicating a message was blinking. *Could it be? Would Sandy have called back already?* There was only one message on their answering machine. All they heard in Sandy's thick southern accent was "Well, I'm not gettin' any younger," and they knew they were on the road to having a child.

When I explain how the story proceeded from there, it often requires repeating several times and illustrating with diagrams. Even though everyone and their mother seems to have gay dads now (ugh, I used to be so special), it is still a tough scenario to compute for many, so don't worry if you need to read over this explanation more than once—you are definitely not the first to be a bit confused and certainly will not be the last.

Once Sandy was on board, Dad and Daddy went into high gear trying to figure out the next steps toward having a family. They had heard from a doctor client of Daddy's that UCLA did artificial

insemination but didn't know if they'd be willing to do it for them. In
the early 1990s it was not very common for two men to have a child
of their own. UCLA got a lot of funding from very conservative and
religious organizations that were not keen on helping the LGBTQ
community reproduce, so there was a huge risk that if UCLA agreed
to facilitate the in vitro fertilization and subsequent pregnancy for
a gay couple they would lose a large chunk of funding. It was not
looking great, but my two sweet dads charged forward nonetheless.
They cold-called UCLA's fertility clinic and told the lovely nurse who
answered the phone their story and desire for a child. She said they
would have to get approval from the board that oversees the fertility
clinic at UCLA as they had never done IVF for a gay couple before,
and, more importantly, they would have to find a doctor willing to
perform the procedure. She gave them a couple of names of doctors
who did those types of artificial insemination transfers at UCLA. My
dads called all of them and only one office called them back. Dr. Caro-
lyn said she would do it, but all four parties—Dad, Daddy, Sandy, and
Auntie—would have to undergo psychological exams, and the women
would have to have physicals performed to make sure everyone was
healthy in mind and body. Thankfully, everyone cleared, and a call
back to those in charge at UCLA was placed to say they were ready to
go! UCLA said the board in charge had approved the IVF procedure,
but under one condition—the parties had to sign a nondisclosure
agreement. UCLA was afraid that if the religious right got ahold of the
news of this procedure and pregnancy, they would try to shut down
their department. However, my dads wanted a child, not to be public
figures at the forefront of the LGBTQ movement, so they signed the
NDA more than willingly. But I'm getting ahead of myself here.

Sandy was initially listed on my birth certificate as my mother and Dad as my father, which would leave Daddy without any legal rights should something happen to Dad or me, God forbid. Dad and Daddy decided they wanted to try to get both of their names on my birth certificate as the two parents. Everyone, my Auntie and Sandy included, had to lawyer up to have the change made. They were told it was the first time in California history that a single-parent adoption had been done for a same-sex couple where one of the child's parents was the sperm donor, his cousin the surrogate, and sister-in-law the egg donor. I believe it was very important to Dad and Daddy to feel like they were both equally my parents, that neither one was "more" related to me than the other, regardless of the biology that created me.

Enough of this biology lesson, let's get back to how I got here in the first place. Sandy moved from Oklahoma into my parents' house, and Daddy gave her a job as an accountant at the accounting firm he owns. Auntie already lived in LA, so she stayed put, but she, Sandy, Dad, and Daddy saw one another almost daily. Now came the not so fun part. Auntie and Sandy had to have hormone shots— mostly administered by my Dad, much to his chagrin. Every day it was Auntie, then Sandy, then Auntie, then Sandy. As a gay man he had never seen so many female backsides on such a consistent basis in his life. Auntie and Sandy's menstrual cycles finally synced up, and they were ready for retrieval of the egg from Auntie and implantation of the embryo in Sandy's uterus. After two painfully unsuccessful and expensive attempts, my parents finally got Sandy knocked up on the third try. They quickly started preparations for the baby. Since it was such a high-risk pregnancy, and because Sandy was diagnosed with gestational diabetes, they got to see me through ultrasounds more often than most parents get to see their babies in utero. I do have more cells now, but to my parents, I am the miracle of those four tiny cells astoundingly turning into a human—a human they named Chelsea Austin Montgomery-Duban.

ⓖ ⓖ ⓖ

My friend, I was created out of what seemed to be an impossibility, and in that I was given a gift. As I've mentioned, I was born with the belief that anything was possible. After all, if I'm here on this planet with a dad who is my biological dad and a daddy who is my biological uncle, isn't anything truly possible? I want to give this gift to you, too, my sweet reader. What would happen if, for just a second, you suspended reality and believed that anything was possible? What would your life look like? What if you were the girl with two dads and a bunch of names? Allow yourself to dream big, because I'll let you in on a secret—you don't need to be the girl with two dads and a whole lot of names because you, just as you are, are enough. Anything is possible for you, too. Now you just need to believe it.

ⓖ ⓖ ⓖ

How would your life look if you gave yourself the chance to believe you are capable of all your heart's desires?

CHAPTER 2

WHEN DADDY FIRST MET HIS LITTLE PRINCESS

"I love you right up to the moon—and back."

—**Sam McBratney,** *Guess How Much I Love You*

ad was prepared for me to be born. He was ready and excited—a father already, just without a child to love yet. He could not wait for the day. Daddy, not surprisingly, considering his dislike of most children, was not so ready for the day I would make my entrance into this world. In fact, I think he may have been legitimately terrified. When Dad called Daddy at his office on July 2, 1993, to say Sandy's water had broken and it was time, Daddy asked if Dad could call him once things were a little further along, to which Dad responded, "Absolutely not. Get your ass over to the hospital."

I did not come into this world quickly. I made everyone wait for my big entrance as I kept progressing and then regressing up and down the birth canal.

Finally, the moment arrived when my little head made its way into the fresh air. Immediately Dad removed his shirt to make sure the first thing I experienced was skin-to-skin contact. Daddy watched nervously from the corner of the hospital room, looking like a kid who had not done his homework and hoping not to be called on. Eventually the doctor noticed Daddy attempting to camouflage himself into the wallpaper and called him out. "You know, Dennis, you can hold her if you want." Daddy nervously emerged from his hiding place. Quietly, in the most tender voice, he asked, "Actually, can I feed her?"

"Of course!" the chorus of voices made up of Dad, Auntie, Sandy, the doctor, and the team of nurses around the room replied. Daddy anxiously took a seat in the rocking chair the hospital provided, and Dad delicately handed me over, their newborn miracle. Daddy took the bottle in his other hand and started very gently to feed me and, as Dad describes it, it was like the part of the Christmas story where the Grinch's heart grows three sizes.

A few days went by and the doctors cleared Dad and Daddy to take me home. While Daddy had gotten more comfortable holding and feeding me, the jarring idea of having to take me home without any specific instructions was terrifying. My Daddy has never even used a coffee machine without first reading every single syllable of the instruction manual, let alone taken daily care of a newborn child. I'm pretty sure he kept searching my onesie for some handy tips and was left sorely disappointed and totally freaked out. Things seemed to get even scarier when they arrived home and I refused to eat. For hours my dads attempted to feed me and I would not take a bottle, no matter how hard they tried. They called the hospital and the doctor informed them that, if in a few more hours, I still was not eating I would need to be admitted to the hospital. Immediately both Dad and Daddy went into a state of panic. They imagined feeding tubes and IV drips all hooked up to my tiny nineteen-inch body. Unsure of what to do next, they called my uncle Robert, my Daddy's brother. He sped over to their house, took me in his arms, and lo and behold, I ate! Turns out I could feel my dads' anxiety—even then, I was an empath. When my uncle Rob took me in his experienced-parent arms, I was at ease because he was at ease, and from that moment on I haven't stopped eating.

After the eating mishap, my dads started to find their groove. Dad did the night feedings, Daddy would get up early for work and sit me on his lap while he watched world news, and I was officially a member of the daddy's girl club. They were an incredible parenting team, but nothing paralleled the way my Daddy loved his little girl.

The moment I was born, everything changed for Daddy, or so he has told me. Once he held me in his arms, he knew his purpose in life would be to make sure, no matter what, that I was safe and warm and that I would come to know what true joy is. Daddy includes these words in his prayers every night. The last thing he always says is "And God, please keep my little girl safe and warm and please make sure that she has self-confidence and is happy, too." He taught me to say prayers as a means of comforting myself when I couldn't sleep at night. He told me to first say thank you for everything I am grateful for and that nothing is too large or too small to express gratitude for —from the tiniest things like a delicious cup of coffee to massive things like appreciation for being alive. He reminds me every day how much he loves me and shows me constantly what true gratitude looks like. It's because of him that I am connected to my gratitude daily and for that I am forever grateful.

ⓖ ⓖ ⓖ

You can use gratitude as a means for coping or celebrating pretty much anything. Whenever things seem to be falling apart, you can tap into the things you're grateful for. Gratitude is an incredible way to also pull yourself out of a bad mood. Even if you can only find one thing, it helps to widen your lens and look at the bigger picture. It's not about ignoring less pleasurable feelings or trying to skip your way out of experiencing tough times, but it's a way to find light within darkness, even if just for a second. It's like a little relief button.

To this day, every morning (well, okay, not every morning, but let's say seven out of ten), I make a quick list of things I'm grateful for. They don't have to be big. They can be anything: a really tasty orange, or a friend texting you out of the blue. You can even keep a running gratitude list that you can come back to at any time. On the days when it's harder to think of something to be grateful for, you'll already have a list of things you can use. Being grateful also attracts more of the things you enjoy and love to you, or so I've noticed in my twenty-seven years on this planet. The more you focus on the things you're grateful for, the more things for which you are grateful seem to appear.

ⓖ ⓖ ⓖ

How would your days be different if you had a running list of everything you are grateful for to come back to in beautiful or challenging (or beautifully challenging) times?

CHAPTER 3

CHELSEA AUSTIN MONTGOMERY-DUBAN

"I am out with lanterns, looking for myself."
—Emily Dickinson

I am insanely proud of my name. I love everything about it and wear it like a badge of honor for all to see. I am not Chelsea Duban. I am not Chelsea Montgomery. I am Chelsea Montgomery-Duban and, if I really feel like making people's heads spin, I am Chelsea Austin Montgomery-Duban. Daddy always says the more names you have, the more royal you seem. So Baby, there's no way I am not using all of those damn names bestowed upon me.

When I was in second grade, my class did a project about our names. We had to research the origin of our names as well as how our parents chose them for us. Since my name was such a big deal to me, this project seemed perfect. When I got home from school I went into my bedroom. I had a little nameplate in my room that I loved and looked at all the time. It was not anything special. Just a blue piece of paper with some flowers on it that slid into a little plastic frame, like a name tag on someone's desk at a call center. I loved it all the same. It was *my* name. *Chelsea, Origin: Old English / Meaning: A Seaport.* I loved that meaning, a seaport, a place where boats come to dock when the seas are rough; a place where people come to find refuge and peace; a day at the sea. I loved all of these pictures in my mind that my name conjured.

I assumed that my parents must have taken a long time, looked through many books, and done much research to find my name. I imagined them poring over baby names together for hours, with cups of coffee (they are always drinking coffee) in hand. I imagined them talking about it with friends and family. How on earth would they ever find a name sufficiently special to label such a special human? As I approached Dad with the question, I was filled with anticipation and excitement to finally hear the story of my name. It was sure to be a fairy tale. I walked into the kitchen where Dad's arms were soapy and wet from doing dishes.

"Dad? Where did you come up with my name?"

"Well, Daddy and I used to have a friend named Chelsea and she was beautiful and kind and a wonderful person. So, I asked Daddy if he liked the name Chelsea and he said yes, so we decided that would be your name if you were a girl. Or if you were a boy it was going to be Nathaniel, but we didn't like the nickname Nate, so we settled on Nicholas because it sounded good."

I stared at him in utter disbelief. That was the whole story behind my name? He asked Daddy, Daddy said yes, and that was it? I was named after a friend they didn't even speak to anymore? What the heck, man! This story was not the magical tale I had imagined. I asked about my middle name, desperate to hear a less boring justification for it.

"Oh, that is a good story," said Dad.

Thank goodness, I thought to myself.

"Daddy and I were at an art fair once and there was an artist painting nameplates. We stopped to watch his work. It was really beautiful. We saw one nameplate he'd already finished with the name Austin on it. We thought it was perfect. And so you became Chelsea Austin. Daddy and I knew we were going to give you both of our last names. We decided Montgomery should go first because of iambic pentameter."

I looked at him quizzically.

"It's something Shakespeare used, you'll learn about it in school one day. It's all about rhythm though. Montgomery-Duban flows. Duban-Montgomery sounds choppy. But we also knew Chelsea Montgomery-Duban is a long name, and at some point in your life, you may want to drop those names, so we thought we would give you a middle name and then if you just wanted to be Chelsea Austin, you could be."

Well, at least the story ended in a more interesting way than it had started. It all made sense and I was still proud. I loved all of my names, even if the story was not as magical as I thought it would be. I went back to my room and started brainstorming how I was going to present my name for the project. How I was going to make it as fascinating as possible. I knew it was already special because of its length and, after a while, the fact that the story that went with it wasn't all that unique didn't ruffle my feathers.

Dad took me to the local Sav-On, where we bought poster board, markers, and TONS of glitter . . . no project of mine was ever complete without a sneeze-inducing amount of glitter flying off the paper. I drew out my name as beautifully as any seven-year-old would, accompanied by every image of the sea and the beach that I could imagine and re-create. The ocean sparkled blue; silly little boats bobbed on the glittering water. I sat back and looked at my name, which took up nearly the entire poster. It made me feel big and important. It was the first time in my young life that I realized names, or labels people give another person, can have so much power to make a person *feel* something. Names, in the form of labels, are impactful. My name made me feel like a princess floating on the water.

Because of my long name, I have been bestowed with nicknames my whole life. No one would ever get the whole thing right and rarely would anyone say it. Most times I would correct them. Very delicately, but I would. As for the nicknames, I became Chelsea MD, which turned into Dr. Chels for some, as well as Chels MD, CMD, CAMD, Chellybelly, Chel, and other combinations. I loved them all—every iteration. Because every nickname or label someone gave me signified that I meant something different to them. It made me feel closer to them. I loved being labeled by people.

☺ ☺ ☺

My friend, my love for labels didn't last forever, though, because the labels or names I was given did not always make me feel like a princess on a sailboat. Sometimes they left me feeling unimportant, unworthy, and like I was being put into a box that didn't make sense for me. Have you ever felt like that? It happens to all of us because people love to understand other people. It's human nature. One way we attempt to figure people out is by labeling them. There are a lot of ways I've been labeled that I love, and also so many that seem to describe everything I don't like about myself. I spent a long time fighting that second category of labels. Then I realized that we have a really incredible power—the power to define our labels for ourselves. Just because the dictionary and society define words one way, what's to say we can't make up our own definitions—more empowering ones—that allow us to feel at home with the labels we're given. We also have the power to reject a label that's given to us or to let a label lead us to an opportunity for growth. Just because someone says we "are" something doesn't mean they know best. At the end of the day, only we know what's best for us and who we are. Don't let anyone else try to tell you that you are something that you know in your heart of hearts you aren't or that doesn't sit well with you. You have the power over your labels even if the rest of the world doesn't know that yet. But don't forget, you always have the power to define exactly who it is you are and who you want to be.

ⓖ ⓖ ⓖ

What would change for you if you took the time to brainstorm labels you've been given and gave yourself an opportunity to redefine those labels to be exactly what you want them to be?

CHAPTER 4

WAIT, BUT DO YOU HAVE A MOM?

"Why do you have to be the same as the others?...
Most of them are stupid."

—**Ken Follett**, *Winter of the World*

There is probably no question I've heard more in my twenty-seven years on this planet than "Do you have a mom?" I've heard it from adults, children, flight attendants, checkers at the supermarket, old ladies on the street, and everyone in between.

My answer is always, "No, I have two dads."

As opposed to saying, "She doesn't have a mom," Dad has always phrased it in a positive way. He never wanted it to be portrayed as a loss or as something negative, and that's how I learned to describe it, too.

Many people, before hearing my response, assume I am a child of divorce and my parents aren't gay, but rather one is my biological father and one is my stepfather. I have started to say, "No, I have two gay dads, and I am biologically related to both of them." It may be too much information for some people, and for a small few it scares them away and they do not know what to say. Fine by me. For others, it sparks a litany of questions—how and why and where and when? These questions were hard to answer as a little kid. Although my family looked different from other families, I did not even know what the word *gay* meant until I was about seven. I didn't understand that there was a specific label for having two dads who loved each other. I had not learned yet just how much the world loves to identify everything until I began my education in society, which wanted to put humans in pretty little, clearly marked boxes.

We were with Daddy on a business trip in Hawaii when I started playing with a little girl in the ocean while Dad, situated safely on his beach towel, looked on from the shade wearing a thick white layer of SPF 70, which he never completely rubbed into his skin. The little girl asked me where my mom was. I said, "I have two dads," and she said, "No you don't," and I said, "Yes, I do."

"No, you don't!" she repeated.

"Yes, I *do!*" I insisted.

She was finally so aggravated that she marched up to Dad and said, "She says she has two dads!"

He responded, "Well, she does."

After a minute of staring at Dad with a quizzical look on her face, she came back into the surf to play, and then we started arguing again. Only this time the words we shouted from the water were,

"Yes, he is."

"No, he isn't."

"Yes, he is."

"NO, HE IS NOT!"

This argument went on for a good two and a half minutes until I marched up the beach and said, "DAD! SHE SAYS YOU'RE GAY!"

Dad responded, "Well, I am."

I thought about this new concept for a moment and then pivoted back to the water, waved to the girl, and said, "Oh, I am so sorry, he *is!*"

This was the first time I had ever heard the word *gay*. I had never thought to ask my dads what they "were" because to me they were just my parents…they didn't need a label for that. Difference is hard to see sometimes until someone else points it out. This little girl, whose name I don't even remember, was my someone else. She pointed directly at my core and said, you are different and here is why. Here is a box with a neat little label on it for your family, please do us all a favor and climb in. But boy howdy, climbing in that box was just the beginning. Everything about my existence was always a question. Don't get me wrong, I appreciate people asking questions and being curious, but as a kid many of the things I was asked weren't things that were top of mind for me and begged quite a bit of rumination and self-discovery on my part.

The only question I have been asked almost as much as whether I have a mom is "Do you miss having a mom?" Now let me ask you, do you miss something you've never had? Do you miss ice cream if you don't know what it tastes like? Sure, you can want to try it, but can you miss the flavor and the sensations? The answer is, and always has been and always will be—no, I do not miss having a mom. I never felt like I was missing a parent or missing some kind of feminine energy around me. I never dreamed of having a mom, either, if you were wondering. It honestly just did not cross my mind. I have been loved so much in my amazing family that I've sometimes thought I would burst. I simply have not felt I needed a mom to succeed in life.

Maybe what people have meant by this question over the years is "What are you going to do when you get your period? Who does your hair for dance recitals? Who is going to teach you how to put makeup on? Who do you talk to your boy problems about? How do you deal with problems two guys won't understand?"

Now, these questions are understandable, and I have a very easy time answering them. As for hair and makeup, Dad got his cosmetology license shortly after graduating from the American Academy of Dramatic Arts, so that solved those problems. At all my dance recitals, Dad not only did my hair and makeup but the hair and makeup of many other girls and boys whose moms and dads couldn't quite perfect it the way my Dad could. He would help sew costumes, and as the only guy on the PTA, he was also the only PTA member who knew how to knit. The issue about who I could vent to about boys was easy, too. To this day, there isn't anything I can't talk to Dad about. I can talk about anything with Daddy, too, though he would prefer to gloss over topics like periods and sex and leave that sort of thing to Dad to handle. If push came to shove, Daddy would always want me to come to him no matter what, but I am still his little girl and it's hard for him to picture me growing up. On the other end of the spectrum, Dad never seemed to feel weird about talking about sex or periods or boys. He was happy I felt comfortable talking to him, and he tried to arm himself with information from his female friends about girl stuff that maybe he did not understand from personal experience. He did everything he could to make me as comfortable as possible and to feel like there was no need to find a mother figure outside our lovely home he had co-created with Daddy.

Now, when it comes to periods and stuff of that nature, as a teenage girl, I was not so keen on discussing my bodily functions with anyone. Dad and Daddy bought me amazing books that explained what girls' bodies go through during puberty. They made sure the house was full of tampons and pads (thank God for you, Dad and Daddy). They armed me with information I could access on my own without having to ask embarrassing questions. I also had Auntie. She and I were extremely close, and while she was not a mother figure to me, I adored her as much as a niece could possibly adore her aunt, and I knew I could trust her with anything. If the need ever arose, she would've been the one to help me bury the bodies, no questions asked. Even with her, though, I did not want to talk about my period. I talked a little bit about it to Amparo, my beautiful nanny, who was and still is one of the strongest female influences in my life. She never made me feel strange, and she came to me before I had to go to her with stuff I didn't want to talk about. Not in a forceful way, but in a way that let me know that these things could be discussed casually—it didn't have to be a parade with banners, baton twirlers, and a marching band, which was more my Dad's style. The bottom line is, I had plenty of people I could talk to and rely on. I had women lined up to be there for me, and I had Dad and Daddy making sure I never felt uncomfortable. I had so many honorary aunties and uncles, as well as blood-related aunties and uncles. I always had someone to talk to, more than I think the usual teenager does. The people I was surrounded by growing up truly understood that it takes a village to raise a child.

So I had two adoring and phenomenal parents and a team of experts lined up for any issue I might come across while going through the sometimes painful process of growing up. The amazing women in my life who have helped me get through so much over the years never tried to be my mom. They never tried to take the place of someone I did not need. I needed a sisterhood as an only child, I needed friends who were older than me to guide the way, but one thing is for sure, I did not need a mom. However, there *was* something else I was looking for.

Around nine years old, I started developing an obsession with families who looked like my family. One day when we were in Mexico for our annual Thanksgiving vacation, Dad and I were playing in the pool when I saw a family who looked like mine. At the time there were no TV shows like *Glee* or *Modern Family* with two dads, so I had to find examples on my own and here was this family in the flesh. Two adorable gay guys with their beautiful children, having a grand old time. Immediately I knew I had to meet them. It was like they were calling to me. The only problem was that I felt a little shy and anxious when it came to these things. I hoped they might come to us if they naturally noticed I also had two dads. I thought maybe they would see my dads and be like "Oh my god, look, other gay people with children, we should be friends." I kept telling my parents to hold hands and kiss each other so the other family could see they were together while I yelled, "DAD" and "DADDY," across the pool at the top of my lungs. Apparently, that didn't work because by day four of our trip, it still seemed this cool family had not noticed us.

After putting up with days of me asking them to "be gayer," Dad suggested I just go over and start playing with the little girls, but that seemed out of the question. Did he really think I could just start talking to them? There was no way on God's good earth I was going to do that. I did not know how to just strike up a conversation. It seemed too awkward and weird and hard to do for my nine-year-old self, so I decided it would be much easier if we ran into them accidentally on purpose. I told Dad to grab one of those big blue floaty air mattress things so I could casually lay on it and bump into them. Dad chuckled, but like he always does, just went ahead and played along. I got myself up onto one of the big blue floaty air mattress things, which is a feat in and of itself, and put my sunglasses on at just the right angle. Then I lay back and prepared myself for our meeting. Dad started to push me across the massive kidney bean-shaped pool to the other side, where the two dads and their little ones were playing, while Daddy, characteristically, lay on a lounge chair tanning and sending emails so we could afford to take vacations like these. I tried to lay there as nonchalantly as any nine-year-old would if they were pretending to be sunbathing. It was nothing but painfully awkward. Writing these words now, I cringe with secondhand shame for my younger self. In hindsight, it definitely would have just been better to walk up and start talking to them, but we were in too deep at this point. I was mustering all the cool elementary school vibes possible to maintain the pretense of merely floating across the huge pool toward, these two guys, who, I'd decided in my head, were super amazing. The pressure was too much to handle. I was too excited and too nervous and too just everything! I started to panic as we started to approach and I noticed them noticing us, which totally ruined the casualness of our charade. I turned to Dad and said, "Abort the plan, abort the plan," and we darted back to the safe side of the pool and out of the sightline of the family I still wanted to be best friends with. Dad thought my reaction was about the funniest thing he had ever witnessed and was laughing hard, which drew attention to us, which of course made it worse for me, so I leaped off the floaty, reached out to cover his mouth, missed, and dove into the depths of the pool, where I guess I thought embarrassment no longer existed.

Later on in the vacation, I finally got the balls to just go over, with Dad in tow, of course, and start playing with the girls. It was strange because once we were playing together everything felt really normal. We had four parents that all happened to be men, yes, but it felt like playing with any of my other friends. I think I expected it to feel different—that there would be some kind of deep knowing that would occur between us. I also realized I had no interest in playing with these children; I was way more fascinated by their parents. I simply felt most at home around adults and I liked finding other adults who were similar to my parents. Moments like these around families like mine were a respite. As much as I enjoyed being the girl with two gay dads, I also really loved these moments where no explanation was needed. This plan was only one of the many schemes I have crafted in my life in order to start talking to gay men. Having two gay dads was kind of my party trick. It made for a lot of good jokes and my dads are insanely cool, so I was one of the lucky kids who adored having her parents volunteer in the classroom or serving as the president of the Parent/Teacher Association, which Dad always was.

I had such a fascination with their gayness. I wanted them to be like the gay guys on television who seemed so much more obviously gay than they were. I wanted people to know they were gay because to me being gay was cool and they were my ticket to the cool kids' table. I always wanted them to kiss in public and hold hands. I wanted them to exaggerate their gayness. I thought none of my friends would know they were gay unless they did these things, and let's face it, my parents were an excellent topic of conversation.

I have realized over time that having gay dads is a little like having parents with an accent. You can emulate their accent, but you cannot really identify what about it sounds different. Dad's mom, Mama, as I call her, is from West Virginia, and even though she has lived in California for over sixty years, she still sounds like she got here from the backwoods yesterday. I love her to pieces, and she is one of the most adorable women ever, with one of the world's heaviest accents. Dad can tease his mom by mimicking her accent perfectly, but when I ask him to describe what her accent sounds like, he says he truly cannot hear the difference in it. I think it's because your mom's voice is just your mom's voice, you know? She doesn't have an accent—it's just how she talks. Well, I guess the same thing goes for my parents' gayness. I cannot really see the more "flamboyant" things they may do. I could not point out the signs that make them "look gay," although everyone else might be able to tell me all the attributes that they say makes it clear for them. I think it's hysterical that it is just little old me who sits and looks at them and cannot quite see what everyone else is seeing because they are just Dad and Daddy to me. Their actions are funny, smart, embarrassing, sweet, loving, and everything else under the sun, but they are not gay actions—they are just human actions, and the fact that my parents are so cool does not have to do with the fact that they are gay. It just has to do with their being cool people who other people, even teenagers, want to be around. They were like icons on my college campus. Before I would even know their flight had landed in Philadelphia, I would get texts from people who went to my school saying, "Oh my God, I just saw your dads! The boys are back!"

I would then call Dad to find out that, yes, indeed, they were on the grounds of my college campus, and on the way to my dorm had been stopped by all my friends, some faculty, and tons of staff, to talk and catch up. I guess I know now that my dads' homosexuality is just one of the many things that makes them amazing humans. It probably would not even be the first adjective on a list someone would use to describe them, though it would be on mine because it is one of my favorite things about them. Just as those people asking me what I was going to do without a mom had not really thought through what they were saying, and how their opinions and questions might affect me, I guess I didn't think about how things might look to the outside world, either.

I also didn't think much of these labels or designated boxes as a kid. I realized, *Oh okay, I guess there is a name for two men who are in a relationship.* I glanced at the box we had been put into, shrugged my shoulders, and moved on. The moving on part of receiving a label is not as easy for me as an adult as it was for little Chelsea, but it's important to find ways to cope with labeling because it seems to be constant in life, even if it isn't always easy to deal with.

In learning to get comfortable with the boxes I have been put in, I have also used this knowledge to better understand people who don't believe the same things I believe or who like to label me differently than I do. They are justified in having their own beliefs, no matter how hateful they may be, because it is what they know. It doesn't make it okay, but I can relate, knowing they are defending what they know just as adamantly as I am defending what I know and cherish. It does not make it right. Ignorance is no excuse for discrimination. It does not make it better, but it helps me to understand other people in the world and to be able to sleep at night. I have incredibly strong beliefs—my family loves to label me "relentless." I am one of those people who, when I set my mind to something, I absolutely will not stop until I make it happen. Like when I was seven years old and wanted a bird and my parents said "no," I did not walk away defeated. I calmly and quietly went into my room and created a ten-slide PowerPoint presentation and accompanying spreadsheet as to why I should be a bird owner and exactly how I planned on taking care of my future pet. Needless to say, the second time around I got a definitive "yes" from both of my parents, but please do us all a favor and don't ask them whether I followed through and performed any of those duties that were actually on that spreadsheet.

© © ©

Regardless of my stubborn nature, I try my hardest to be open to all points of view. In this polarized world, we are taught to despise and be afraid of what we do not know. It's not that we should be blind to what makes us different, but this polarization makes it so hard to have relationships and understanding across political parties. Before we've even begun a discussion, our belief that the "other side" is wrong is a foregone conclusion. I used to think that, as a radically liberal person, I owned the label open-minded. Well, it turns out I was open-minded if you agreed with me on issues about LGBTQ rights, abortion, the environment, racism, sexism, and the list goes on and on. I realized that just because I am liberal does not mean I am open-minded. I was shutting down other peoples' beliefs because they did not line up with mine, and sometimes I did so out of self-preservation. As you can imagine, it's really hard for me to debate my family being a legitimate family. However, I found that we have an opportunity in being vulnerable and open with people who are different from us. When we show someone who we are, it's easier to understand why someone is the way they are and build something beautiful where before there may have been disgust or hatred. Polarization drives us apart but I believe we are meant to come together. We are meant to better understand each other and become more open-minded in every sense. We should celebrate our unique backgrounds and the things that make us each special. To live as if we do not see things like race, religion, sexual orientation, gender identity, level of ability, or class would be to miss out on a celebration of beautiful people and cultures. Where we find openness in ourselves, we find endless opportunities.

So, I ask you, my friend, what is the worst thing that could happen by opening yourself up to someone who is vastly different from you? How might your life be different by opening up instead of closing off when you feel that someone may have different beliefs than you do?

CHAPTER 5

OATMEAL FACES AND TRIPS TO LAS VEGAS

"How do you spell 'love'?" —Piglet
"You don't spell it, you feel it." —Pooh

—A. A. Milne

D addy has always been a very busy man. Even before I was born, he was busy creating the perfect life. The image of the man I remember as my Daddy from childhood is a man with a mug of coffee, spiky black hair, and some form of palm pilot or cell phone in his hand at all times. Daddy is a certified public accountant—the most phenomenally genius CPA ever and the only one I think I've ever met who actually loves accounting. When he realized that, as a gay and Jewish man, he would never be able to work his way up in one of the "Big Eight" accounting firms (now the Big Four after several of the largest accounting firms in the country merged), he opened his own firm back in the 1970s and built it from the ground up, with his own two hands and a calculator. The Big Eight accounting firms had expectations like that you would have a wife and play golf, neither of which he was particularly interested in. Daddy is not someone who had things handed to him. He worked hard for everything he has and ended up making something really incredible. Daddy is insanely smart, was top of his class at USC, and even won the Forbes medal for getting the top score out of 30,000-plus people on the CPA exam the year he sat for the test. So, yeah, seriously smart.

Daddy was hard on himself, convinced that he alone would create the perfect home. A home where Dad and I would never have to want for anything. He accomplished that, but it came at a cost. Daddy worked all hours of the day and on every vacation we ever went on. This is one version of Daddy that I hold in my memory, but he has another side to him as well. There were many occasions when he would drop everything to be with me. It did not happen often that Daddy and I had uninterrupted time, but when we did, it was magical.

Daddy is the kind of father who makes everything more fun and I think he invented the phrase "go big or go home." When I was a wee one and did not want to eat my breakfast, he would design a face on my oatmeal with fruit so it would look more appetizing. He also taught me to love fine dining. Every Thursday from the time I was five until I was in double digits, Daddy would take me out for "father/daughter date night" while Dad went to his choir rehearsal. Daddy always made it a special occasion and even if I was just a little kid, he picked the fanciest restaurant he could find because that way the meal would, in his words, "last longer so we would have more time together." In these moments, his work never came with him, and he was there for just me, and I knew that for sure. We would talk about everything, from the kids in my class to how attractive I found the waiter to what kind of vacations we should plan. When Daddy was with me, he only had eyes for me. He would, and still does, look at me as if he were constantly memorizing my face, making sure to take in every expression.

My parents owned several income-producing properties in Las Vegas, and I know this may sound strange, but Daddy would take me to Vegas once a year to check on the properties with him, even when I was a baby. It was our special trip and I grew up with a different idea of Sin City than most people have. To me, it was a place where Daddy took me to Build-A-Bear by day and Cirque du Soleil, magic shows, and Celine Dion concerts by night. We ate amazing food (I've always had quite the palate for fancy dishes) and spent time wandering around, watching the fountains at the Bellagio froth and burst high into the sky. That was my Las Vegas. I did not understand gambling, hated the smell of cigarette smoke in the casinos, and didn't know why so many people were having so much trouble walking straight. This place was the magical land where I got Daddy's undivided attention. If he worked on these trips, it was never during the hours when I was awake. He would wake up before the crack of dawn to take care of any emails and stay up to take conference calls long after I lay my head down on the pillow so he could spend the entire day just focused on me. These days were some of the best days of my childhood.

Not only was Daddy insane amounts of fun, but he was also my champion. In Daddy's eyes I could do absolutely no wrong…much to Dad's chagrin.

On more than one occasion when Dad was trying to discipline me, Daddy was standing behind him, contradicting him, and making me laugh. One time when Dad was really laying down the law,

Daddy stood behind him waving his arms and mouthing, "I don't know what he's talking about! You're perfect!" Finally Dad caught sight of him in the glassy front of the microwave and, without moving a muscle, exasperatedly exclaimed, "I can see you!" I'm not saying directly contradicting your spouse in front of your child is necessarily the most helpful thing for you to do as part of a parenting team, but boy, if there is one thing I could be sure of, it was that Daddy would always, *always* take my side when it came to anything. He is not the person I go to when I want an honest opinion about a haircut or an outfit because he will always tell me I look beautiful, and I know he really believes it, too. When I want brutally honest advice I go to Dad, because man, oh man, does he know how to dish that out like candy, but Daddy would stand by me no matter what.

My Daddy showed me what it looks like to love a person without a single condition, with your whole heart and soul. He gave me the courage to accomplish anything because he showed me that you can be a nerdy kid who is brutally bullied in school and turn your life into something spectacular. He illustrated for me what it means to make a fairy tale out of a life that felt far from it. He taught me that my drive and passions were greater than my fears and that there is not anything I am not good enough for. He is an example for young people everywhere who feel they are worthless. He persevered and made the life he wanted, and if he could do it with a calculator and a lot of gumption, you can do it too—just set your mind to it, put in the work, and believe.

ⓖ ⓖ ⓖ

My friend, when I look back on these stories of my Daddy, it also is striking to me how when he gave me his attention, he truly did so one hundred percent. His mind may have been at work, but to me it felt that he was really there and present with me. No emails. No calls. Just time for the two of us. It is not often these days that we really take time to put down all of our electronics and just be where we are. We are so caught up in posting things the moment they happen or in instant gratification that we struggle to be present with the ones we love. I have a deep appreciation of showing those you love that you care about them by putting down my phone and really being with them when I have the chance, which is definitely something I learned from my daddy subliminally on these trips to Las Vegas. When I bring my whole self and the person I'm with does the same, it means more than any words could express. I often feel cheated when I sit with a friend and they are half there, the other half making plans for later, checking Instagram, or posting stories in real time. Life is too short not to appreciate the time we have together whether it's documented on the 'gram or not.

ⓒ ⓒ ⓒ

What would it look like to give someone 100 percent of your attention when you're with them? How might that change your relationships?

CHAPTER 6

SOME PEOPLE HAVE SECURITY BLANKETS. I HAVE LISTS.

Life is what happens to us while we are making other plans.

—Allen Saunders

As I've mentioned, I have many aunties and uncles in my life. Most of them I am not related to by blood, and Auntie Melanie is one of my most special chosen aunties. She is everything I have always wanted to be when I grow up. Gorgeous inside and out, clever, devilishly funny, spiritual, and uncompromising of who she is. Although I am pretty sure she would never describe herself in those terms, it is how I have always seen her.

Auntie Melanie has known my parents since before I was even a thought, and so I have never known life without her. Auntie Melanie walked into Daddy's office about a decade before I was born. She was referred by another client because who wouldn't want my adorable genius of a father doing their taxes?

The day they met they hit it off. Daddy is not someone who loves to socialize. He talks with clients all day long at work, so when he comes home, he just likes to have a good meal with his family, watch some TV, and go to sleep. So, it was quite a shock when Daddy called from the office to tell Dad that they just absolutely had to have dinner with his new client, Melanie Wilson. Dad (the social director of our family) called Daddy's new client, a total stranger to him, and invited her over for tacos. She politely accepted, and they became fast friends. Now, back to two decades later, and the part that involves me . . .

From my understanding, Melanie never wanted any kids of her own, but she was very maternal, taking me under her wing as if I were her niece or daughter. One of my favorite things about her was that even when I was itty bitty, she talked to me like an adult. She took what I had to say seriously and always treated me with respect. She never belittled my drama with other kids or boy stuff. She thought I was worthy of listening to and when she listened to me, she really listened, considered what I had to say, and gave only the most thoughtful of responses and advice. She was, outside of my parents, the only person I called at least once a week while I was away at college. She was someone I could talk to about my parents when I was frustrated or mad or sad or disappointed, and even though she was their friend first, it was our little secret, and it never stopped her from loving me or my parents any less.

When I was six, my separation anxiety was at its peak. The thought of a sleepover was utterly terrifying, which is why my parents thought that maybe sleeping over at Auntie Mel's would be a good stepping stone before staying at a friend's house.

The scariest part of a sleepover was the sleeping part, so I made a schedule before I went to Auntie Mel's house that we were to follow.

It was designed to change activities in half-hour increments and went all the way until eight in the morning so I could avoid sleeping at all costs. Dad and I met Auntie Melanie for lunch, then I took my mini red and green rolling suitcase out of Dad's car and Auntie Melanie drove me to her house. I was really nervous, but I knew if I just followed my schedule, everything would be okay. When we arrived at her home, I showed Auntie Mel my detailed itinerary. She did not comment on the fact that it allowed no time for sleep but rather told me it was a great plan and that she was happy to go along with every item on my agenda. Immediately, I felt comforted and relaxed, assured that this was all going to be alright. We started the second we stepped into her place. First, we played with the marbles she'd collected over the years, then we organized said marbles, then we organized the marbles in a different way. Then we had a snack. Then we read a book. Having babysat my fair share of kids by this point in my life, I look back at Auntie Mel with the utmost admiration. I cannot believe she went along with every single thing and didn't even drag her feet through the process.

When it was time for dinner, something weird happened. Auntie Melanie's boyfriend, Todd, came over. I did not know Todd. I did not particularly like Todd, and most importantly, Todd was not a part of my plan. I let him stay through dinner, figuring he would leave shortly thereafter, and we could get back to the scheduled programming, but he did not seem to want to leave. He even brought me a book in an attempt to win me over, which I politely thanked him for, and then I requested to speak with Auntie Melanie privately in the kitchen.

"Auntie Melanie, Todd is not on my schedule," I said.

Since she is the most remarkable human being ever, she promptly told Todd that he had to go. I also took a moment to let Auntie

Melanie know that I did not think Todd was right for her, and her now-husband, Bill, thanks me for my ridiculously blunt nature at six years old.

We were able to get back to my schedule—finally, playing every game and discussing every subject I could possibly think of. We were approaching four-thirty in the morning, and when I saw Auntie Melanie was getting tired, I became alarmed. We still had so many things left on the schedule! She asked if we could sleep for just a few hours and then get back to the schedule, and I begrudgingly acquiesced. She said she just needed until eight o'clock. I was exhausted, yes, but my fear of sleeping away from home was stronger than my need for sleep, so at about seven fifty-nine, I got as close as I could to her face without actually touching her and stared, willing her to wake up. I hated and still hate waking people up directly, so I always have found inventive ways to do it. I figured staring at her would do the trick, and I was right. Auntie Melanie popped out of bed much more pleasantly than I deserved, and we went downstairs because the next thing on my list was to make hot cocoa. Now, not having given Auntie Melanie a copy of the schedule prior to my visit (rookie mistake), she was not adequately prepared with hot cocoa powder. Nonetheless she, of course, saved the day by having chocolate chips and milk, and we attempted to make a hot cocoa of sorts. We had a yummy breakfast, and moments later Dad was there to pick me up, and I ran into his arms. I was so happy to see him but so sad to leave Auntie Melanie. He promised I would see her again soon, and off we went so that she could take a nap, and I could make some more plans.

Before I left for college, I asked Auntie Melanie if we could have one more sleepover together. She showed up at my parents' house ready with a schedule of activities in half-hour increments for us to follow. The tables had turned in the most beautiful way. That time we got a bit more sleep, but not much—after all, we had to stick to the schedule.

© © ©

For those of you who also struggle with control issues, I feel you. It makes it really hard to feel okay when plans change. It's not easy to roll with the punches. Us control freaks love things to be planned out and to know exactly what is going to happen. Unfortunately, that just is not the way life works. Everything is always shifting on its axis and the whole world—and even us, it seems—is changing. We can have as many plans as we want, but we have to find a way to be okay when things veer off the deep end. The surprises—both good and bad—teach us lessons and contribute to the beauty of life. We don't have to be afraid of falling off balance because we will get back up, maybe even learn a thing or two, and sometimes we can even get back to the plan we had in the first place.

© © ©

What would life look like if you let go of controlling every little thing? Or when things went awry, you were able to look back and find a lesson?

CHAPTER 7

ONE PERCENT

"And always, there was the magic of learning things."

—Betty Smith, *A Tree Grows in Brooklyn*

I grew up in schools where it was actually cool to be smart. I have heard so often that as a kid, when you're intelligent you are shunned, or considered nerdy. (I think nerds are awesome. Also, I totally am one.) In the schools I went to growing up, or maybe it was just my friend group and I didn't realize it, we prided ourselves on getting good grades. Studying hard for a test wasn't bookish, it was just the thing to do. When you got good grades, you were one of the cool kids—well, maybe cool is pushing it. Either way, in my group of friends it was important that you were intelligent, and by intelligent I mean getting A's on tests. I was not a great test taker when I was growing up. I didn't always do well on tests and I was someone who had to study harder and longer in order to do well. Book smarts didn't seem to come as naturally to me as it did to my friends.

Starting in kindergarten, I had three best friends: Isabella, Hailey, and Alissa. We were inseparable. We went to school together and danced together every day. We ate lunch, played at recess, and did everything as a foursome. When Alissa moved away in second grade, it was hard on me, although it was also secretly a relief because she was one tough cookie who constantly seemed to put me in uncomfortable positions. After my very first sleepover (the one at Auntie Melanie's house), I had a sleepover at Alissa's house. She tended to be moody and halfway through the sleepover decided she didn't want to talk to me anymore. I did not understand why. There was no reason or explanation, just silence. I tried and tried to get her to say something to me, and she would not budge. I ended up spending most of my time that day hanging with her mom, who just brushed it off as Alissa being Alissa. (Maybe that was the beginning of why I seemed to relate to adults so much more easily?) So, yes, I was sad when she moved to a faraway state but also grateful that I would not be at the mercy of her mood swings on a daily basis, and, thankfully, I still had Isabella and Hailey.

Now Izzie and Hailey, they were smart. Don't get me wrong, I was, too, but I had to work much harder at my schoolwork than they did, or so it seemed to my little elementary school self. We were besties, but we were also insanely competitive inside and outside school. Each of us was spurred on by our own unique home situations. I wanted to please my parents more than anything. Izzie's dad had ridiculously high standards for his young daughter. Hailey's mom was not always easy to track down.

One time, when we were in second grade, our teacher was handing out the latest tests after having graded them. I waited nervously at my desk, fidgeting with my pencil box as I wasn't so confident that I had passed with flying colors. Our teacher walked up and down the aisles of desks until she stood right in front of me with a big smile on her face. The test lay face-down in front of me, waiting for the moment of truth when I would turn it over and accept my fate. I breathed the biggest sigh of relief when I saw a big gold star at the top with "Great job! 99%" written next to it in my teacher's swirly handwriting. I was flying high. It felt amazing. The acknowledgment that hard work pays off, even for my seven-year-old self, was just the bee's knees. Izzie, who was also in my class, turned around and asked me what grade I got. I proudly whispered, "I got a 99!" thinking my friend would be so happy for me. Turns out, she got 100 percent. She looked at me disdainfully and remarked casually, "See, so that just shows I'm one percent smarter than you." I looked at her for a minute with puppy eyes, confused, my little head cocked to one side. Why was she saying this? Wasn't she my friend? She started giggling, and so I did, since I was not really sure what to do. All the same, it hurt. *One percent smarter,* is that what the test was telling me? That we are all ranked by smartness based on the percentage we achieve on one test? That could not be, but there it was right in numbers. And numbers are indisputable. I went home to Dad after school and cried. I was so sad. I was 1 percent less smart than Izzie, and I could not stand the feeling. Dad was horrified by Izzie's behavior and wanted to call her mother right away, but I told him not to. I wanted to fight my own battles or not fight them, but either way, I didn't want Dad to embarrass me in front of my friend. I would settle for being 1 percent stupider. I didn't want to argue.

In fourth grade, Izzie and I were in different classes, but the percentage difference in our intelligence, or at least my perception of it, always pushed me to try harder. A certain group of kids from my class were invited to work outside school on a higher level of math. I was not one of them. Of course, Izzie was part of the group.

When I got home the day I found out, I told Dad, "I want to be a part of the harder math group. I think I can do it if I really try, but they didn't pick me."

Dad, busy making dinner, called over his shoulder, "Why don't you just ask Ms. Winokur to let you try?"

That idea had not occurred to me. I hadn't thought that maybe I could advocate for myself and ask to be a part of this special group, and maybe, just maybe, they would let me take part. I walked into school the next day, beyond nervous, arriving fifteen minutes before the bell so I could talk to Ms. Winokur in private. At just about five feet tall, she was one of the most inspiring teachers I ever had. At ten years old many of us already towered over her. She bounced around every day in pigtails and purple velvet overalls, and I thought she was the coolest. She made learning fun. Photosynthesis was really fascinating when she explained it, and if ever there was a teacher who would give me a chance, I knew it would be her.

"Good morning, Chelsea! How are you?" she asked gleefully, as if she was made of caffeine.

"Hi, Ms. Winokur. I'm good, thanks. Um, I have a question."

"Sure, Honey, what is it?"

Sensing the seriousness in my tone, she pulled out two chairs so we could sit down next to each other.

"Well, I know you gave some of the other kids an advanced math book. I know I didn't get one, and I know I'm not the best at math, but some of my friends are teasing me about not getting one, and I was wondering if I could try the higher math group?"

Ms. Winokur smiled the most heartwarming smile you can imagine. "You know, Chelsea, you're good at a lot of things and people are always good at different things. I'm sorry if anyone is teasing you, and

I can absolutely talk to them about it. The math book is very advanced and math isn't your strongest subject, but if you want to try, you certainly can. I just have to talk to your parents about it."

Knowing my dads would, of course, say I could try, I nodded my head vigorously. I didn't care how hard it would be, I would study as much as I needed to. I just wanted the special green math workbook that all the smartest kids had been carrying around. That day after school she gave me the book and told me what they had done so far. I opened the workbook to do my pages of homework, so incredibly proud. I looked at the first page and thought, *Oh geez, she wasn't kidding, this is hard.* Negative numbers? I had never heard of those numbers before, and why, when you added them to positive numbers, did they get closer to zero? I was going to have a lot of catching up to do, but I was up to the task. I took extra time on my homework. I asked questions. I kept up, and later, when it came time in middle school to take a math placement test, I tested at the highest level. I could push myself out of my comfort zone and do things other people thought were beyond me. Take that, public school trying to put me in a box! Unfortunately, honing my math skills, while making me more confident academically, did not exactly help in the friendship department.

Izzie and Hailey would constantly gang up on me or leave me out. They would hide my math book from me so I couldn't get my homework done or they would hide in the corner of the playground and tell me I could not hang out with them, which only made me love them more. I wanted to be as cool as them, a part of their club, but try as I might to study them in order to be cool, I never had success.

One time on a field trip to a pumpkin patch, Izzie's mom was chaperoning. Izzie and I were sitting on a prickly bale of hay and eating lunch when she suddenly got up and walked over to her mom. While I was still in earshot, she yelled, "Mom, I just can't be with her all the time. She's driving me crazy!" I knew she was talking about me, and so did Dad, who was also chaperoning and happened to be standing next to her mom. I stared down at my sandwich, trying to pretend I didn't hear, tears stinging the corners of my eyes. My dad walked over and sat down on the hay bale next to me. He wrapped his arms around me and I buried my face in his chest, finally letting the tears fall.

"I'm so sorry, Baby. Maybe it's time to play with some other friends," Dad suggested.

But I didn't really want other friends. I wanted my current friends to be better friends and to like me as much as I liked them.

After that, I started hanging out with Dad and the other adults on field trips. They just seemed to understand me better. When I was in third, fourth, and fifth grade, since the kindergarteners had a different lunch schedule, I'd volunteer in those classes during my lunch time instead of eating with the other students my age, so I wouldn't have to deal with the torment that went along with having friends. The teachers of the classes I volunteered in were nice to me, and I liked the kindergarteners, so I didn't mind. As I started to grow up, I realized I tend to suffocate people with my love. Izzie's words may have been the first, but they would not be the last to call me clingy and annoying. I didn't understand how to love people just enough, but not so much that it made them crazy. I began to train myself to find people who didn't get sick of me and my brand of love and to give people space. When my best middle school friend told me I texted too much and tried too hard, I tried to care less. I succeeded in texting less, but caring less just was not in the cards for me because it felt good to care.

It turned out that it was mostly adults who were compatible with my kind of friendship. As a result, my best friends growing up were my school teachers, dance teachers, and friends' parents. They did not just tolerate me, they enjoyed me and appreciated me the way kids my age didn't. On the other hand, those friendships were not quite right either because adults always had things they could not say or could not share with me because I was "too young." I spent my childhood bouncing around in half friendships with people my age and with people twice my age.

No one really got me like my parents. They knew what it felt like to be outsiders and so when their little girl felt like one, too, they knew how to give me a home where I could be myself and be loved and where my love was appreciated. They treated me like an adult. I did not get the kids' menus at restaurants, I did not act like a kid, and so they did not treat me like one, either. Until college, our home was the only place where I really felt I fit. Everywhere else I was like a puzzle piece that you tried to jam into place, one that kind of works where it is, but you know it doesn't really belong there. Luckily, I always had a friend here and there who I could count on, especially at dance class.

But, to rewind back to elementary school, before I could find my people, I had to learn an important lesson: how to stand up for myself. Easier said than done. I thought I would have more friends if I did what people told me to do and followed them around like a puppy.

Izzie and Hailey would tell me, "If you go to the playground and run around the field twice and then go to the handball courts and wait for us until we tell you to come out, we'll be your friends."

They were literally making me run after their friendship. I was scared to respond the way I needed to, but Dad had told me if I could be brave, they would respect me and maybe stop treating me so hurtfully. So I looked at them and said, "No!" I didn't have the courage to say anything else, but I managed to get that word out of my mouth, and they looked at me, their mouths agape. They didn't understand who I was. In that instant, I had my power back. They may have walked away from me in that moment, but in moments to come they would not torture me the same way they had. A silly smile crept across my face when I realized I was in control of how other people made me feel. Izzie and Hailey didn't end up becoming lovey-dovey, amazing friends, but they didn't make me perform for their friendship or their love anymore. They were just my friends although we remained competitive, as was a part of our nature.

Interactions with them were just the beginning of my understanding of what it meant to stand up for myself and believe in what I have to offer as a person. Dad would remind me that when I didn't like the way they were treating me I should speak up, but also that I should know in my heart that everyone is going through something, and they may take it out on me because I am a nice person. It did not mean I had to put up with it, but it would help me understand where they were coming from and know their anger had more to do with them than with me. He told me to say a prayer for them, send them white light and love, and hope things would get better. And I learned the truth of this, that people's words often have much more to do with them than they have to do with the person they are saying them to. I know this to be true because of LA traffic. The things I shout at drivers from the safety of my own car have a lot more to do with me being mad at myself for leaving late than they do with the person I don't know in the car in front of me. Go figure!

⊚ ⊚ ⊚

My friend, as I look back on these friendships, I see that these girls weren't really my friends. They were asking me to perform for their love and in essence prove my worth, something that has landed me in therapy over and over again. It's always easier to see in hindsight when we are putting up with more than we should. However, we have an opportunity to learn, in these scenarios, about what we are willing to put ourselves through and what we are worthy of. It turns out we are all worthy of wonderful friends who don't make us prove our value and who do support us in our decisions and life. You are worthy when you wake up in the morning without having to do a single thing. Friends who don't make you feel loved and enough are not worth having. Walk away and find the people that fill your cup with love, gratitude, and abundance. Friendship isn't perfect. Stuff will come up, you will disagree, get angry with each other, and sometimes even hurt each other unintentionally, but you should never allow people to take your power and make you feel like you're worthless because you, just as you are right now without changing a thing, are enough.

⊚ ⊚ ⊚

How would it feel to surround yourself with humans who make you feel worthy? How can you bolster those relationships and start letting go of toxic relationships in your life?

CHAPTER 8

IT'S TIME TO POP THE QUESTION

"Sometimes the questions are complicated,
and the answers are simple."

—Dr. Seuss

We were in Hawaii as so often happens in the story of my life. Daddy had a boatload of clients in Hawaii, so Dad and I got to go quite often as freeloading, lei-wearing, lounge chair–sitting tagalongs. On this trip, it was just a few weeks shy of my tenth birthday. Dad and I had spent all day at the pool while Daddy worked, and then we went to dinner at one of our favorite restaurants, Kyoya, which sadly no longer exists. It was one of those cool Japanese restaurants with tatami rooms, where you sit on the floor and take your shoes off. Everyone ate in their own private room separated by paper walls, and it felt very traditional (please note my limited knowledge of what traditional Japanese culture is). Lovely kimono-adorned waitresses glided in and out of the wood-paneled walls and prepared your shabu-shabu at your table. Kyoya was pretty freaking cool—maybe one of my favorite restaurants of all time, actually.

I had been thinking all day about asking my parents a question, a question I had been mulling over in my mind since I was about three. Back then I had asked, "Where did I come from?"

Dad answered very literally, "a tummy."

"Whose tummy?"

"Sandy's."

"Did she want to give me up?"

Dad gave me a loving, somewhat worried look. "Oh my goodness, of course not, Honey. See, Daddy and I wanted to have a child very, very badly, but in order to make a child you need a part from a boy and a part from a girl and a baby grows inside a girl, so we asked Sandy if she would help and she said yes."

This explanation seemed plenty for my three-year-old self and I was satisfied with that answer for a long time.

Four years later, when I was seven, I asked my parents about sex, and then things got kind of confusing because if they needed a boy part and a girl part, I started wondering was the girl part from Sandy? Was I actually Sandy's baby? Where did the boy part come from? Was it her husband? Was I not related to my parents at all? *Where did I come from?* was not a question with a straightforward answer like it was for most kids. There was some explanation I was missing, but I was a little too shy to ask, and I am not even sure I knew what I wanted to ask.

Two years after receiving the sex talk, I was nine and had been mulling over these questions for a good long while, so I decided the night at Kyoya was the night I wanted to ask my parents. It was so strange. I had never felt uncomfortable asking them anything. Did I feel so weird because I was worried my parents would be questioning whether they were my real parents or not? Was I afraid to hurt their feelings? We sat down to dinner and I waited until we had ordered and had our food so it wouldn't be quite as likely that we'd be interrupted. I had been very quiet, which was highly unusual for me, and my parents looked at me expectantly as I looked down at my plate and as if I was just curious about the ice cream we may or may not have later said, "Um, I was just wondering, can I ask you guys a question? How did you guys have me?"

They looked relieved as soon as I asked the question. It was not like me to be so shy in front of them. Later, I learned that they had concocted every possible idea of what might be going on in my head and were terrified but didn't want to push me in case I didn't want to talk about whatever it was.

They looked at each other excitedly and then back at me before responding, "Oh, Sweetheart, we were wondering when you would ask." Then things got a little crazy. They explained the process to me, how they had used Auntie's egg and Dad's sperm, and that Sandy had carried me. I remember the feeling of complete elation that took over my body in that moment. Not only was I related to both Dad and Daddy by blood, which was important to me (I have a mild obsession with my heritage), but also Auntie, whom I had always felt inherently connected to, was actually my biological mom, and that was one of the coolest and most exciting things I had ever heard. From the time I was a little girl, whenever she walked into the room, I would squeal. As I got older, I only ever wanted to sit next to her at family dinners. When we went to Disneyland for my birthday, I would insist that Auntie come even if all my guests were a bunch of five-year-olds.

Every time Auntie was near, I got an excited feeling in my tummy and
my chest. This nine-year-long mystery was finally solved, and it was
everything I could have ever dreamed of and more.

   It made sense now when people told me I look like both of them.
The hushed conversations that had gone over my head as Dad and
Daddy explained things to other adults in the room finally all fell into
place. My dads were relieved, too, as they had not been sure how I
would react to learning about all of this. It turned out that Auntie had
also been stressing over this conversation since my transfer at four
cells. She had wondered if I might be mad at her because she hadn't
kept me as one of her own children. For me, it was just the opposite.
I felt loved and cared for by everyone, and I felt I fit perfectly in my
family. Daddy immediately called Auntie on his silver flip phone with
the little antenna to tell her the good news. I told her it was perfect,
and I loved her so much. That night was one of the highlights of
my childhood. We went out and celebrated over banana splits and
laughed and held hands everywhere we went. We were the three musketeers and life was unicorns and rainbows. I found out later that if I
had not asked about how my parents had me by the age of ten, they
were going to sit me down and tell me because they thought it was
important for me to know. I guess somewhere in my mind I knew it
was the right time, and I was thrilled to have found out the way I did:
on an island, over shabu-shabu in one of my favorite restaurants, with
the two best guys I know.

☺ ☺ ☺

*It can be such a challenge to be honest in situations where the stakes feel
so high, like all of these times I asked about how I came to be. What I*

deeply appreciate about my Dad in these moments is that he has always been straightforward with me. Whether it was for an honest opinion, or an answer to a question. I used to really struggle to give honest opinions and answers to questions because my need to please people was somewhat overwhelming. I just wanted them to be happy, who cares about the truth, right? Wrong. After watching my Dad for so many years be brutally honest with people, I saw how respected his opinion became. It can be hard in the moment to speak honestly and from the heart, but I trust my Dad implicitly because just as he answered my questions about sex, or gave me an opinion on an unfortunate haircut, I always knew I could believe whatever it was he said and that he would never lie to me. We all have someone like this in our life. Someone we know we won't ask a question of unless we want to hear the truth. But when we have the strength to be that person for others, even if we sugarcoat things sometimes, it creates trust and respect in a relationship.

© © ©

How does it feel when someone gives you an honest opinion? What if you were that person for other people? How would that make you feel?

CHAPTER 9

A GOVERNMENT WORKER AND A GIFT FROM GOD

"Reserving judgements is a matter of infinite hope."

—**F. Scott Fitzgerald,** *The Great Gatsby*

A t twelve, I had my first run-in with the law. Well, not really law enforcement, just a passport control officer, which is a part of our law enforcement that still scares the living daylights out of me. My life growing up was pretty perfect, but to say we didn't face occasional discrimination when we left our shining little home would be a lie. When I was twelve, we were coming back into the country from a delightful family vacation in Italy. I was tired and jet-lagged, and I just wanted to go home. The lines were long, as they always are at LAX, the nation's most depressing airport (it truly makes me sad that it's the first thing tourists see when they come to LA). Finally, we were called forward to the immigration console. We had nothing to hide, there was no reason to be nervous, but as the immigration official kept staring at our papers and flipping back and forth in our passports, we all started to get a little restless. These people are trained to make you feel nervous even when you have not done anything wrong. I hate that.

After what seemed like an eternity, he looked up and said, "You need two forms, you aren't a family."

We looked at him, somewhat perplexed, trying to figure out what he meant. He was then so gracious as to clarify for us, "You guys aren't married; therefore you aren't a family."

We stood there, dumbfounded. *Was this imbecile really telling us that we weren't a family?*

He was clearly getting agitated that we were taking up so much of his time. He said as if it was nothing, "Look just go and fill out another form and tell her that she has to pick whose form she wants to be on."

Now, that was the last straw. This stranger who knew nothing about us was asking me to choose one form to be on. Filling out a customs form may not seem like a big deal, but for me, that meant choosing Dad or Daddy. That meant disowning one of my parents just because they could not legally get married—I guess the thing in America that makes you a family. My family was everything to me! I was so scared and did not understand what was going on, and I was hurt that the label of what we are didn't fit in their box, so they wanted to force us to change just to fit. My dads tried to comfort me as I cried, but I was inconsolable and they were embarrassed that we were going through this ordeal because of a silly customs form. They showed him my birth certificate, which says parent and parent with both of them listed, but he just kept shaking his head.

I was crying so hard that something had to burst, and it turned out to be my nose. Right there in the middle of passport control at Los

Angeles International Airport, I proceeded to get the world's most massive nose bleed. I mean, blood *everywhere*. It looked like someone had punched me in the face. Other immigration agents were sent to find me some gauze and some water, and the immigration officer we had been working with was so overwhelmed and caught off guard that he looked at us completely speechless for a moment and then said, "Oh, never mind, just go," and stamped our customs form and let us back into the country.

Right then and there I realized how arbitrary and subjective the law can be. The definition of family at that moment was decided by one angry old white dude who was clearly exasperated by the horrific ordeal he had to go through, letting my family of three American citizens into the UNITED States of America. I get sad every time we go through customs to enter the U.S. The way customs officials treat people, especially those who are not American citizens, is incredibly upsetting to me. I don't like the way most customs officers speak to the people they interact with. Just because someone does not speak English perfectly does not mean they are less intelligent. It is actually much more common for individuals not from the U.S. to speak multiple languages than it is for Americans to know additional languages. Whenever I see a customs official speak unkindly to someone, I want to scream from the line as I wait with my passport in hand, "We're not all like this! Welcome to the United States! I hope you have a nice time and meet kind people!" Sadly, I don't quite have the balls to do it, since I don't really want to be hauled off to some room to be questioned, but I am thinking it. I wish there were more humanity, understanding, and kindness when it came to those who are put in positions of power, no matter how little, over other people. I have found more often than not that people are doing their best and that there is a story behind every face. If we took the time to learn those stories, or at least acknowledge their presence, we would all be more accepting, loving, and well-rounded individuals.

I was aware from a very young age about why this discrimination was happening. My parents were always sure to tell me that it was because having two dads wasn't the "norm" and so sometimes people don't understand. I was so proud of my family though, and being the daughter of two such incredible parents, that it would upset me that other people didn't "get it," but none of this ever made me wish that I had a more "normal" family. To me, my family was perfect. This experience at LAX was one of *many* times that we've had uncomfortable interactions with customs and immigration as an LGBTQ+ family and there were always things my parents had to do and go through that most parents don't. We never left home without my birth certificate, just on the off chance that while crossing the border somewhere my dads would be questioned about where my mom is and face scrutiny and questioning as if they were abducting me. This happened once crossing the border to Canada. One time in the Bahamas, my parents tried to explain to an immigration officer that I was their daughter and the woman thought it was so ridiculous she just started laughing uncontrollably and asked my dad to please stop explaining because she couldn't take it before she eventually waved us through. They also traveled with a complete file that showed all of my history in order to connect both Dad and Daddy to me since they weren't legally married at the time. We didn't go anywhere without lots of paperwork.

ⓒ ⓒ ⓒ

My friend, we are all on this planet to learn, grow, and change. My parents were worried before they decided to have a child that being the kid of two gay dads would be too much of a burden to bear for me. Then they realized that everyone has some sort of challenge in life and that maybe this would be mine. And I think it's true. I highly disagree that having two dads is a burden; maybe it's caused me to have to explain myself more than most, but that doesn't bother me so much. What it has taught me is that we never know what anyone is going through. We don't truly know anyone's story unless we are intimately connected to them, yet we love to judge people quickly and harshly from the outside. Seeing the way people react to our family's presence, especially ten and fifteen years ago, has made me pay so much more attention to the way I react to people. What it has taught me is that we can start to try to catch ourselves every time we make a judgment about someone because we simply do not know their story. From the person who cuts us off in traffic, to someone standing in line that just irks us at the grocery store, we can try to catch ourselves in these judgments and remind ourselves that we don't know their story because chances are, if we did, we would likely have more empathy. Sometimes it's not about never passing judgment, it's just about catching yourself in the act so you can make a new choice and change your thought pattern about people you know nothing about—for your sake and theirs.

◎ ◎ ◎

What is something you've gone through when you wish someone wouldn't have passed judgment? How can you take that knowledge and extend that grace to someone else?

CHAPTER 10

DEATH IS RIDICULOUSLY MESSY

"People will forget what you said,
people will forget what you did, but people will
never forget how you made them feel."

—Maya Angelou

D eath is really complicated and really messy. I think every parent has a fear of the moment they have to face the issue of death with their child for the first time. Luckily for my parents, I made it easy. When I was three years old, my favorite food was sushi—yes, I was even a basic white girl back in the '90s. We used to go to the same sushi restaurant several times a week, where the sushi chef taught me how to suck salmon roe through a straw. My dads were utterly horrified, but I was as happy as a clam.

One day we sat down at the sushi bar and I ordered my favorite deep-fried soft shell crabs—I know, I was a freak of a three-year-old with a crazy palate—and the efficient Akio, the sushi chef, brought them out. Only thing was, they weren't yet fried. Akio picked them out of the container with his chopsticks and there sat four little live crabs crawling around the sushi bar.

I looked at Dad, and I looked at the crabs, and I said, "I'm gonna call that one Fred!" Dad, Daddy, and Akio all had looks of sheer terror on their faces. Akio said to Dad, "Do you think she still wants them?"

Dad shrugged his shoulders and mouthed, "I guess so?"

So off went Fred to the deep fryer. My parents were panicked for the moment when Fred came back on a plate, no longer crawling around. They saw the chef coming with my plate of crabs, complete with a lovely dipping sauce, and they braced for impact. Their gentle, animal-loving little girl was about to have her first brush with death and an understanding of where her food came from.

I took one look at the plate, looked at Daddy, and said, "I think I'll eat Fred first."

My parents almost split at the seams with relief and laughed uncomfortably for a good few minutes.

Sometimes, though, death wasn't so funny.

When I was four, my parents gave me a puppy for Christmas to teach me responsibility. What it taught me was that if you wait long enough to take care of the dog, Dad will do it for you, so let's say the most I ever did for this doggy was love it unconditionally. I adored Teddy, whose full name was Edward Crosby Cavanaugh (let's face it, the dog had two gay dads, too; he needed a fancy name). All I wanted was for Teddy to love me. Except we had one little problem. Despite his adorable good looks, Teddy was a touch fear aggressive, and he would launch himself at you teeth first, as if he were rabid, if you tried to get close to him. I would lie next to him, feed him treats, give him all the love I could muster, and he would still snap at me. Although, on occasion, he would love me, too. He'd let me read him books, he'd listen to my problems and never try to solve them, and most of all he kept my secrets. So no matter how tortured and difficult this little pup was, I loved him. The fact that he didn't want me in his face only made me love him more. (I guess playing hard to get really does work.) He calmed down in his old age, and just as he started to love everyone a little more and started to freak out a little less, he was diagnosed with throat cancer. I was devastated. He was my little guy. No matter how crazy he was, he would always be my puppy.

When I was seventeen, Teddy was diagnosed with cancer. My parents invested in every therapy possible. We were determined to save our little guy. For several weeks he went through treatment, but it was clear he was struggling and getting weaker every day. One night, while he was at the vet recovering from his most recent treatment we got the call we had been dreading. The phone rang late in the evening during a lovely dinner party my parents were hosting to celebrate our friends visiting from across the pond. The clinic did not think he would make it to morning, and they thought it would be more humane to put him to sleep. Dad asked me if I wanted to see Teddy before he passed.

Up until that point, I had never lost anyone or any pup close to me. I knew I had to see him, just once more. Dad and I made our excuses and left Daddy pouring wine and attending to our guests. When we got to the clinic, they gave us options: We could either say our good-byes and then they would put him to sleep, or we could hold him while the procedure took place. Dad was horrified at the prospect of his daughter holding their dying dog in her arms while they put him to sleep, but I was adamant. I wanted to be with him. I wanted to hold him and comfort him and thank him for years of secret keeping. So, they put us in an oddly Pepto-Bismol pink room, with very calming lighting on a very uncomfortable futon, and brought in my little guy. He was wrapped in a pink blankie, and when I looked into his eyes, they were already glazed over. I knew he was not really there anymore. His soul was off ready for new adventures in doggie heaven.

As they got ready to put him to sleep, I said, "Don't worry, it's the same stuff they gave Michael Jackson."

The vet tech looked horrified, but Dad laughed and I giggled and I knew Teddy would have appreciated the joke, too. He had quite a sense of humor. The experience was not scarring. It was magical. Being there to put his soul to rest gave me the chance to let him go, to know that he had a bigger name on the other line, and it was his time. I cried a lot that night and I knew getting over the loss wouldn't be quick, but when I woke up in the morning and felt the Teddy-sized hole in my heart, I also knew he was safe, and he was warm, and probably less tortured than he had been by his nightmares on earth.

Death is a crazy thing and we all have to process it differently. I am grateful to my animal angels that helped me first discover my way of processing death and realizing it is a transition and not an end. They helped me have a healthy relationship with death because it seems to be the one inevitable thing on this earth. So, it is best to learn how to deal with it in a comfortable way for yourself as soon as you humanly can.

ⓖ ⓖ ⓖ

In the ten years since Teddy's passing, I have experienced much more loss. It seems to happen more and more often as you get older, which makes sense, but each time it is a fresh wound.

It's so important to understand that there is no right or wrong reaction to a passing whether it be of a family member, friend, or pet. We all have this expectation that grief should look a certain way and I am here to tell you that I have grieved several times over my twenty-seven years and not once has it looked the same. If you don't cry at all, that's really okay, there is nothing wrong with you and it doesn't mean that you didn't love the person you lost. If you cry nonstop, that is also 1,000 percent natural.

Honestly, I tend to process death with a lot of humor and that can make people really uncomfortable, but it's something that works for me during the grieving process. The best thing we can do around loss is to stop judging our own and others' reactions to death. Grief looks different on every one of us every single time. Let's give ourselves space to breathe while we process instead of adding more pressure of processing a certain way. If you want to go to therapy, amazing. If you want to talk about happy memories, great. If you want to hole up in your bedroom for a while and just be on your own that's okay, too, but don't forget, even in the midst of horrific loss, there are people who love you and an incredible world out there that's waiting for you when you feel like taking that next step.

And one more thing, when someone is experiencing loss, I ask that you never use the phrase, "I understand" or "I know," in reference to their pain because, to be honest, none of us can know anyone else's pain. We only know our own and saying you know or understand can undercut the pain someone is feeling.

If you are currently experiencing a loss, I am so very sorry. My heart is with you. You will get through this. And tell all those people, including me, to stop throwing freaking platitudes like "they lived a long life" your way, it's annoying as hell. I believe in your ability to get to the other side. I really, really do.

ⓒ ⓒ ⓒ

How can you give yourself more grace when you are experiencing an unfavorable emotion? How might that aid in the grieving process or just in letting that emotion pass through you?

CHAPTER 11

THE TRAUMA THAT IS BEING THIRTEEN

"I did everything he did,
but backwards and in high heels."
—Ginger Rogers

I got my first period when I was thirteen. I was pleasantly relieved to know that I was, in fact, becoming a woman and utterly horrified at the same time. There is a strange kind of pride in getting your first period, which is exciting and also a little terrifying because your body is involuntarily bleeding, except it's not supposed to be a bad thing, it's supposed to be a beautiful thing, and these things are just one too many things for a hormonal thirteen-year-old to be feeling. It all feels like a bit *much*.

I remember being in the bathroom the morning we were leaving on another trip to Hawaii and looking down at my panties to see what I was sure was a sign of womanhood. I quickly stuffed some toilet paper in my underwear, pulled up my pants, and tried to figure out exactly what to do next. First things first, I opened up the cabinet under the sink and grabbed the boxes of tampons and pads Dad and Daddy had bought years before in case of emergency, and then quietly pulled the books they had provided that talked about how to handle these bloody shenanigans off my bookshelf. I walked back to the bathroom with my stash of goodies in hand and sat on the toilet, holding a book in my left hand and an unwrapped tampon in the right while I read how to insert said tampon, and I just gave it a try and shoved it up there.

I was grateful my parents had supplied me with pads and tampons preemptively so I did not have to tell them right away. It was so much to process on my own, and, frankly, it was messy and a bit embarrassing, even though my parents were encouraging me to be 100 percent open about it because they thought it was an amazing thing. Them thinking it was such an amazing and beautiful thing was also terrifying because I would have rather it just not be happening in the first place. On the other hand, it was exciting to know that I was catching up to some of my friends and the thought that maybe I might get boobs soon was also pretty enticing (P.S.: despite fourteen years of periods, I am still waiting for mine to come in). I tried to just deal with it on my own, since I was feeling shy. I wanted to hide in a dark room where no one could find me, but somehow when you are trying to hide because you're utterly embarrassed, life has a way of forcing you out of your dark little corner.

We got on the plane to Hawaii. I sat on the oddly warm leather seat squirming around, uncomfortable and anxious that I would stand up with a red stain on my dress, so I just avoided standing up at all costs for the entire six-hour flight. Paranoid that someone was somehow going to be able to read it in my eyes that I just got my period, I stared down at my lap and read a book for school as I sipped my juice and prayed to God that I could get through this plane ride without any major embarrassment. And I was lucky. My first period was not so painful or heavy on the first day and so I just prayed and prayed to get to the hotel room where I could quietly process how the heck I was supposed to feel about all of this. I got through the first day pretty much unscathed. And then, the next day, we went to the swimming pool. Or what I think of as a torture device for young women on their very first period.

My parents had really had done their best to learn as much as they could and give me a million books on becoming a young woman, all of which were very helpful, but certain things are not in those books. Things that say, "Hey, you have to change your tampon when you get out of the pool, especially if you have a heavy period." So, I was swimming in the pool while rationing my tampons, knowing if I ran out of them that I'd have to go to my parents to get money to buy more, and they would, of course, want to know what was going on. I got out of the pool and sat down on my lounge chair and then I felt something weird. I now know it is the utterly horrifying feeling of your tampon overflowing. However, I did not know what it was at the time. I did not know how to get to the bathroom discreetly without showcasing my newly found womanhood to everyone in the pool area, so I just hoped nothing was going to happen when it was time to go to lunch.

As I stood up, wearing my little pool cover-up, I noticed the lounge chair I had been sitting on was stained with blood. Not a lot, but enough to draw attention and to need a new towel. Not sure what the game plan should be, I threw another towel over the chair and continued on behind my dads. Only the problem was, my bathing suit was wet, and your period doesn't have the courtesy to say, "No worries! I'll hang on until you're in a bathroom where you can handle this all very discreetly!" No—it just forges on ahead. Next thing I knew the chair cushion at the hotel restaurant was soaked, as was my cover-up. A very kind waitress, who had known me since I was little, came up and told me that perhaps I should go to the room and change because it looked like I was having an accident. Okay, now what is more humiliating than that? Not only do your parents notice, which would not have been so bad, but now all the hotel employees you know have also noticed and the attention of the guests is also directed at you, and it's a shit show of epic proportions for a thirteen-year-old who just wanted to handle all of this growing up stuff on her own.

It is almost as if the Universe was telling me not to go it alone, and then when I did not want to take its advice, it decided to take matters into its own hands. After that debacle, my parents were so sweet and so helpful, and I was still horrified and embarrassed. The thought of leaving the hotel room made me want to cry. Dad encouraged me to call Auntie—the one who donated the egg so my parents could have me. I told him I didn't want to. I did not want to talk to anyone about this. He told me he really thought it would be helpful if I talked to a woman who could assist me with handling my newfound womanhood. I refused and refused, but much like me, Dad does not take no for an answer. The next thing I knew, I was talking to Auntie, and she was helping me through all of this mess. She explained about using tampons: change it when you get out of the pool; don't sleep with one in. Use pads if you're not comfortable with tampons. She recommended her favorite brands of everything and made me feel normal about it. Not embarrassed, not ashamed, not even like it was a big deal, and I was grateful for that. Because, as adorable as my dads were, looking at me adoringly and telling me how proud they were of me for becoming a woman, I just really didn't want attention drawn to any part of me. Auntie made me feel taken care of but also let me know it was just normal and made me feel welcome to the club without going through any grueling membership process.

© © ©

My friend, girls don't necessarily need a celebration of their womanhood when the strangest thing in life thus far is happening to them (at least in most cases). Yes, it is an amazing, beautiful thing and no girl should feel uncomfortable talking about it and celebrating it if that's what they want, but also, when you feel like someone is squeezing you from the inside out and you're bleeding for a week without dying, sometimes you want to just hide in a hole and let the world go on without you for a couple of days. There's nothing wrong with that either.

What I'm getting at here is, you do you. In any time of your life, whether it's getting your period, or getting into college, celebrate or don't celebrate in any way you want to or need to and feel free to be honest with people about what you want and need. You deserve to be honored in the manner in which you desire. Sometimes people have the best intentions and yet they muck it all up. It is okay to ask for what you need at any point in your life. Actually, it's more than okay, it's wonderful! It is also okay to be disappointed when people don't celebrate you the way you hoped they would. Ask for what you want and need (this one is a real relationship saver). No one is a mind reader so don't expect your friends, family, or partner to know exactly what it is you want. Whether it's needing space, a kiss on the forehead, or wanting a McDonald's Quarter Pounder in the middle of the night, you are worthy of asking for and speaking your truth out loud. You don't need to make yourself smaller to make other people happy.

ⓖ ⓖ ⓖ

How can you find ways to start asking for what you want and need in your life? How might that look?

CHAPTER 12

MISTAKES AREN'T IRREVERSIBLE

"A woman is like a tea bag—you can't tell how strong she is until you put her in hot water."

—Eleanor Roosevelt

We all do stupid things sometimes. When I was in high school, I wanted to be liked by everyone, which I have since learned is virtually impossible. One of the most common currencies in high school is gossip, and if you have gossip on someone and you share it, that tends to make you more popular. I was not immune to this concept. One time I was hanging out with a group of girls at lunch (I went to an all-girls high school, so saying it was a group of girls is redundant), and we were sitting by the lockers gossiping. Funnily enough, there was one girl in our class whose mother had dated Daddy some thirty years prior (obviously my Daddy was still in the closet back then), and to be perfectly honest, I did not like this girl much. She was very blunt and sometimes not so nice to me, which gave me what I felt like was license to make up a story about her. I did not have much to offer to the group, so I told everyone that this girl could not stop talking about how our parents dated, and how annoying she was, and how she was so desperate to be friends with me. The girls around me were all giggling and eating up every word I said, when all of a sudden, I heard a voice from around the corner that said, "You know I'm sitting right here, right?"

I was horrified. This behavior was so unlike me. I was not the gossipy type and I didn't know what had gotten into me. My desperation to be liked and included in the cool club got the better of me. At that moment I knew I had two options: I could run away and pretend nothing happened or I could walk around the corner and apologize.

I waited just long enough for the shock and horror to subside and then I walked around the corner and said to the girl, "I am so sorry. That was horrible of me. I should have never said those things and I know they aren't true. I am really, really sorry. Can I give you a hug?"

Much to my surprise, she actually let me give her a hug, and she told me it was okay. I promised to make it right and to tell the other girls that what I had said was not true, and I vowed to myself to remember the horror of that moment any time I thought about making up lies about someone else to gain favor with other people. I still felt awful. I knew I had to talk to Dad about it, and I was terrified. I knew this type of behavior would not fly with him. I thought he would be pissed and, worse, disappointed in me. In fact, I was sure of it. I ran to the bathroom to call him with a pit in my stomach because I knew I would not be able to wait until the end of the day to tell him what had happened. I thought the guilt might actually eat me alive. I sat in a bathroom stall and started sobbing while I dialed. This may have been the only time I broke a school rule, using my phone during school hours, but the urgency of the situation, to my mind, seemed to usurp any kind of policy. It was such a stupid thing for me to do, so mean and small-minded. I knew I was in for a tongue lashing.

Dad picked up the phone, confused by my call in the middle of the day, and I told him the awful things I had said and that I had immediately apologized for them. Much to my surprise, he did not yell. He told me it was okay and I could hear that he actually meant it. He said we all make mistakes like this, and I did the right thing by immediately apologizing and setting the record straight for this poor girl. He told me I learned a valuable lesson and he was pretty darn sure I'd never do the same thing again now that I understood how horrible it felt when you were caught in the act. "The truth will always come out," he said. "You can't hide anything forever, so better to just deal with the consequences immediately when you do something wrong rather than bury it because you will never get away with it anyway."

He was right. No matter how tiny a lie you might tell, someone will figure out that you are lying, and your cover will be blown. And when a lie is going to affect someone else's life, you'd better think twice before you say it. I may have an overactive conscience, but the way I felt that day will always sit in the back of my head as a reminder of what it feels like to hurt someone else and how it's better to fix it right away than to bury it and run.

◎ ◎ ◎

Here's a little nugget for your thoughts. It is a really icky feeling when you know you have done something that has hurt someone else. I tend to want to apologize over and over when something like this happens because I feel so horrible—especially when someone doesn't accept my apology—which happens. But here's my feeling: once you've owned it and apologized, don't let it burden you. You did the right thing by correcting your wrong. Do not let the guilt haunt you forever or let anyone make you feel bad for doing a "bad" thing. You have owned it, you have apologized, and if everyone cannot move on, then maybe you just need to move on without them.

ⓖ ⓖ ⓖ

What would you tell a friend who felt they had messed up and apologized and their apology hadn't been accepted? How can you treat yourself with that same grace you would give a friend?

CHAPTER 13

HERE COME THE GROOMS

"Love is patient, love is kind. It does not envy,
it does not boast, it is not proud. It does not dishonor others,
it is not self-seeking, it is not easily angered, it keeps
no record of wrongs. Love does not delight in evil but
rejoices with the truth. It always protects, always trusts,
always hopes, always perseveres. Love never fails."

—I Corinthians 13:4–7

I always wanted my dads to get married. I am not sure why I had this obsession. I loved that my family was different, but marriage, now that was a sticking point for me. Maybe it was because, even when I was a little girl, I knew my parents were denied a right, or really, hundreds of rights, that I thought they should have. As I got older, I realized all of the things marriage means beyond just bonding two people. It allows you to visit a hospital after hours as a family member. There are tax and employment benefits and many other perks that you get as a married couple, which you do not receive as a couple in a civil union. Anytime marriage became legal anywhere in the world, I begged Dad and Daddy to get married. When it was legal in Vermont, I thought we should go there, and then in Massachusetts, then anywhere in Canada, then New Zealand. I was desperate; I just wanted them to be married. Then, on a glorious day in 2008, same-sex marriage became legal in the state of California. I thought, *Man, there is no way they can pass this up now!* But they told me, "Chelsea, we're a family. We don't need a piece of paper to define us."

"I know," I said. "But if you're going to ask for equal rights as part of the LGBTQ community, then you better exercise them." Because what is the point of equality if you are not going to exercise your rights? Finally, after days of negotiation—everything is a negotiation in my family, unless it comes from Dad and then it's straight-up law—they said yes, they would get married. After twenty-six years of being together, they thought if they were really going to get married, they were going to do it right! They only had six weeks to plan the wedding. Same-sex marriage was up for a test on the 2008 election ballot in the form of Proposition 8, which could potentially ban it, so they had to move quickly. They enlisted the help of only the most fabulous wedding planner, Charley Izabella King, who is a goddess if I ever met one. My little fifteen-year-old self would look at Charley and just dream that I could be like her when I grew up. She was a striking British *glamazon*, who had performed in the West End and on Broadway, and she put together the most stunning wedding anyone had ever seen at lightning speed.

I can remember it like it was yesterday. I could barely sleep the night before; I was so excited. I got to the venue with two friends of mine, even before my dads did. I wanted to eke out every second I possibly could of the day. (You would have thought it was my wedding . . .) My dads spent the day getting ready on a separate part of the estate in Malibu where the wedding was going to be held, and I made them wait until the very last second to see me in my new hot pink gown that I was going to give them away in. I had butterflies all day, and I wasn't even getting married! Finally, at six o'clock, as the guests took their seats, we met behind the massive gray stone building that hid us from family and friends. Daddy welled up at the sight of me in my dress. There he was, once again, memorizing my face. Then Dad and Daddy locked eyes and spoke in a silent language they'd perfected over the years to say, "After all this time, here we go on our next adventure."

At least, I really hope that's what their eyes were saying. I stepped up between the two of them and the three of us linked arms, a position that has always been natural to us, the three musketeers. We watched as all four of my grandparents walked down the aisle, and then it was our turn. Watching my parents exchange vows from the sidelines, I could not help but feel overwhelmed with emotion.

My parents exemplify what love is, I thought. *How could anyone say this kind of love or any kind of love is wrong?* However, after months of watching protestors, and even some of my family members, condemn gay marriage, I knew the fight was not over. Nonetheless, just like we always have, we ignored what everyone else might think and went on being ourselves and loving love.

There was not a dry eye in the house for the entire ceremony. These two men who loved each other so deeply were finally able to legally do what so many others had been taking for granted for centuries.

When it was my turn to speak, I was beyond nervous but incredibly excited. I broke down halfway through. I could not believe how happy I was. This was the moment I had envisioned for so many years. This was the moment, to my mind, when everyone would start to see us as a family, even though we had already been one for decades (take that, stupid passport control officer). This was the moment. This was the dream. In case you're wondering what I said that left everyone reaching for tissues, here it is:

"According to me, marriage is not just a man and a woman or two people who love each other and promise to be together in sickness and in health. And marriage is not even a beautiful white dress. But what marriage really is, is love blossoming between two individuals and a promise that what they have together can only get better. Marriage is a bond between two people who love each other so much their hearts are bursting with joy and love and compassion for each other, and no one can tell them they don't belong together, or that they shouldn't love each other.

"My parents are a perfect example of this. Yes, they work hard at their marriage, but they also love each other more than anything in the world. I cannot believe anyone could think Dad and Daddy should not be together because there are no other human beings in the universe more meant for each other and happier than they are. They are my dads, my role models, and I hope I am one-tenth as happy as they are when I find someone to spend the rest of my life with."

I looked out into the audience exuding love and excitement for our little family. It filled me up and left me thinking, "What therefore God hath joined together, let no man put asunder" (Matthew 19:6). Okay, well it probably didn't leave me thinking that at fifteen since I'd never opened the New Testament, but still, that was the overall sentiment.

On election night 2008, my dads and I sat staring at the TV in total disbelief. After all the progress the community had made, after all the decades of effort, we watched the legalization of same-sex marriage in California melt away. We had all worked so hard. We had all made such a difference. My parents were disappointed, yes, but they weren't devastated like I was. I felt like my heart had been ripped out of my chest. My teenage mind could not comprehend that anyone would think it would be a bad idea for my parents to be together. It was astonishing, astounding, and downright frightening. I felt like I did not know my neighbors anymore, that there were traitors all around us, that people we knew must have voted against same-sex marriage or it would not have passed. I felt betrayed by everyone I thought I knew and by my country. I was deeply and personally affected by what other people had done in no more than two seconds in a ballot box.

My parents were never the "let's wave the rainbow flag and convince everyone that gay is the way" kind of people. They were more the "let's just live by example and change minds" sort. However, after Proposition 8 passed, I knew I had to do more than just live. That was not enough. I had to wave my rainbow flag even if it meant putting my family at risk of criticism by the outside world. Better these people criticize us out in the open than behind closed doors. So, I put the video of my speech from my parents' wedding on YouTube. I hoped it might change just one or two minds. I hoped that maybe a few people might look at the video and see how much I adore my parents and think, *Wow, how can this whole gay thing hurt us anyway?* I put myself out there to stand up for a community I believed in, whether they wanted me there or not.

Turns out, people did want me there. Somehow Perez Hilton got ahold of my video and retweeted it, skyrocketing the views overnight.

I remember my dad calling me over to his computer and exclaiming, "I don't know what happened, but your video has 50,000 views!"

I was in total disbelief. I hadn't expected that at all. Before I knew it, the *Miami Herald* was calling me for an interview. I even spoke at a Pride Month event for Toyota. Everyone seemed fascinated by this girl with two dads who was willing to speak out about a community she loved. I was more than excited about the prospect of speaking about my family to anyone who would listen. It seemed like the perfect opportunity for people who were unsure about the whole "gay thing." I also faced a lot of internet trolls. People become very brave behind a screen name and a keyboard.

It was an amazing lesson in not letting what people say about you get under your skin and speaking your mind. I had comments ranging from "You're all going to get AIDS and die" to "They aren't your real dads. Go to hell." Lovely, right? But somehow, I knew the purpose of me sharing this video was bigger than that because I was also getting messages from young gay teens who needed support and were looking to my dads and me, and from people who said they didn't understand why gay people wanted marriage equality and just why it is so important. I also knew that there were so many people whose minds were shifting and changing that I hadn't heard from. But beyond all of the comments, I knew in my heart of hearts that I had done what I felt to be the right thing. I followed my heart, and thus far in my life, when I have truly listened to what my heart wants, it has never steered me wrong.

☺ ☺ ☺

My friend, it's easy to let the bad comments outweigh the good, but we must try to focus on the positives. My Dad has always said, "Negativity yells while positivity whispers." I think it's time we flip that script and start to find ways to scream positivity (when it's genuine). It's time to give more clout to those endorsing our worth and who we are and to let the rest go. It is in our human nature, I think, to tear people down in order to make ourselves feel better, especially when we're feeling low. We do this subconsciously, but when it sneaks out into the open it can be so hurtful. The negative comments that people spew are not about you, they are a reflection of how they feel about themselves, so let that shit slide right off your back. Don't get bogged down in the negative. Yes, take constructive, kind criticism, but the stuff that's just negative for negativity's sake or being used to hurt shouldn't take a moment of your time. You deserve better.

ⓒ ⓒ ⓒ

The next time you encounter someone else's negativity affecting you what is another way that you can look at the situation? How might that new perspective empower you instead of bog you down?

CHAPTER 14

DREAMS, TELEPROMPTERS, AND MARIE ANTOINETTE

"The core of authenticity is the courage
to be imperfect, vulnerable, and
to set boundaries."

—Brené Brown

Every year since I was twelve, my dads and I went to the very formal Los Angeles gala for the Human Rights Campaign. It was and still is a who's who of the LGBTQ community. I would watch all these people speak and talk about how they could change the world, and shockingly enough, even as one of the youngest ones there, I was inspired and not put to sleep. I always had a secret dream that I would get to stand up on that stage and make a speech of my own. I wanted to truly make a difference in the world for the community that raised me. I wanted to make their lives less fraught, I wanted them to see they could have more families like mine. Especially at the time, I wanted everyone to be able to marry whomever they loved, if that was what they wanted.

I had this little dream every year when I watched the speakers, all pretty famous actors, singers, or politicians, never really seeing how it could happen for me. Then, miraculously, the speech I gave at my parents' wedding went viral. Notice was taken by people and publications all over the world, and people from around the country were asking me for interviews. They wanted to know the sixteen-year-old girl who had two dads and was a spokesperson for gay marriage in the United States. One day Dad called me while I was at dance class, which was weird because he never called when I was there.

"Hey, Chels, do you have a second?"

"Yeah, sure, what's up?"

"Well, Honey, I have an exciting question—do you want to speak at the HRC dinner?"

For a moment I wasn't sure I'd heard him right.

"What? Are you serious?" I squealed.

I got so excited I started screaming at the top of my lungs about how thrilled I was. It was only a week away. I would have a speechwriter who would send me a draft, and I would be reading off a teleprompter. One of my very biggest dreams was coming true. I was going to be speaking at the same event as Portia di Rossi and Senator Barbara Boxer.

Since I am an overachiever, I had many rehearsals for my upcoming dance recital, classes, and a mountain of homework to get through before the event, not to mention I had already planned on taking the SAT for the first time the same day as the gala, a mere eight hours before I would be speaking in front of a whole room of strangers.

That Saturday, I walked into Malibu High School to take the SAT.

It was a school campus I did not know at all, which already made me nervous, as I'm totally panicked about logistics. Luckily, I had two friends with me: strength in numbers, right? By the way, have I mentioned that I hate standardized testing? It causes me so much anxiety because I feel like I'm not good at it. I always got close to straight A's, but there was just something about those damn standardized tests that got the best of me. I would get nervous and freak out and not be able to concentrate if I did not understand something. It's not like a test you can study for in school, where you make sure you know all the information and then go take the test. It's a combination of all these things that you may or may not have learned by the time you are in eleventh grade, and you hope to God you get a good enough score to get into the schools you want, knowing all the while that you are so much smarter than you will ever look on one of those tests. Regardless, it's a part of the process if you want to get into those schools, so I played the game and I went in and took the test. I tried desperately to stay focused—the little dots on the Scantron slowly eating away at my psyche—but honestly, how could I focus on this stupid test when I knew in a few short hours I would be in the midst of one of my greatest dreams of all time?

I left the SAT and put it behind me, knowing if it really went as badly as I imagined it had, I could always take it again. I ran to my car and rushed home so Dad could take me to the hairdresser to have my hair done for the gala. I could barely sit still. I reviewed my speech over and over again. I had never worked with a teleprompter before, and I was pretty freaking nervous. I went back home, put on the same dress I wore to my parents' wedding, and off we went.

We were way overdressed, but we did not care. My dads were so proud and I was so excited. Someone who worked for the organization came up to us and said, "What did you do? She looks way older than sixteen!" The whole point of me speaking was to get people to donate money inspired by this young girl of sixteen, so they were going for a younger look than the way I looked in my fancy clothes. Oh well, the asking for money was a side note for me. I was most excited to share my story and maybe even open some minds—even though I knew I was preaching to the choir. Maya, the kind woman who was helping me navigate the event, took me into the ballroom so I could have a sound check and practice working with the teleprompter. I got up onstage and started reading. The text scrolled faster and faster—I couldn't keep up!

I looked at Dad, who was standing in front of me, and said, "Dad, why is it going so fast?" My voice was shaking, my heart was pounding, and I was on the verge of tears.

He smiled at me and said, "Honey, it goes as fast as you. If you slow down, it will slow down. There's someone backstage listening to you and operating the machine. Just go at your own pace and they will follow."

Well, no one had told *me* that! I didn't know how all of this technology worked. Once I got the hang of it, I walked off stage and we went outside to mingle and wander around the silent auction area.

The venue was quickly filling with beautifully dressed people and all of a sudden it hit me: I was going to be speaking in front of a crowd of almost a thousand. Oh. My. God. A thousand people— *What the heck was I thinking when agreeing to this?* When we sat at our appointed table as the main event started, I stared down at my dinner plate, unable to eat. I kept asking Daddy what time it was. I was almost comatose. Daddy kept asking if I was okay, and I could see him motioning to Dad over my head that he was worried I wouldn't be able to make it through the night without imploding. The event coordinators were used to working with celebrities and politicians, people who did this sort of thing all the time. They were not used to working with a nervous sixteen-year-old who liked to know all the logistics. Logistics made me feel safe. I wanted to know when I would go backstage, where it was, who would take me. I wanted to know everything.

Dad didn't have the answers, which horrified me, but I found out soon enough when Maya came to collect me from the table. Dad said I looked like Marie Antoinette on the way to the guillotine. My head was down, and I could barely breathe. I am sure Dad and Daddy almost had a heart attack thinking their girl, who was never nervous onstage, was suddenly paralyzed by the thought of walking out onstage and speaking. They didn't care what happened, as long as I wasn't disappointed or embarrassed—they kept telling me that over and over—but I could not hear them. They sat in the audience, waiting for it to be my turn.

Backstage, everyone was so nice to me. Joe Solomonese, the former president of Human Rights Campaign and a friend of ours, was there. I didn't know him well at the time, but as soon as I saw him, I knew it was all going to be okay. He hugged me and told me I was going to be great. I am pretty sure the words that ran through my head at that point were *"If you say so."*

Katy Perry's "Teenage Dream" started playing, and I heard Tim Morneau and Anton Mack, two HRC champions, announcing me: "Straight from taking her SATs just this morning, please welcome Chelsea Montgomery-Duban."

That was my cue and out I went. Shockingly, even with paralyzing stage fright, I felt so alive. Everyone was clapping and whistling;

it was like they all knew who I was. It did not stop me from shaking in fear, but then I did one of the most courageous things I think I have ever done. I stood there, took a deep breath, and admitted to the crowd of people how I was feeling. I said, "Oh my gosh, I'm so nervous. I'm literally shaking right now." And something magical happened. Everyone laughed, and immediately I felt like the bubbly, funny, entertaining Chelsea I really am, not the paralyzed-with-fear, thinking-I-will-throw-up Chelsea I was just moments before. Then it was easy. I had everyone in the room on my side. Determined to soak it all in, I began. It could not have gone better. I could literally feel the energy of the room shift. I made them laugh. I was able to tell everyone about how I had been attending Human Rights Campaign dinners since I was twelve and had always had a dream that I would have the opportunity to speak at one myself. I talked about my two sweet dads both of whom I am biologically related to. (Cue the excited gasps.) I also learned how to sell. Ultimately, my job was to pitch why people should donate to HRC and it turned out I was a great saleswoman. I got people to donate a ton of money and everyone was happy.

Exiting the stage, I saw my dads at the bottom of the stairs, waiting for me, chests puffed up and full of pride in their perfectly tailored tuxedoes. I was beaming. I felt like I was on cloud nine. It was one of the best experiences of my life.

As I approached the bottom of the stairs, someone ran up to me. She said, "You were so wonderful, one of the best speakers I've ever heard. You should be so proud of yourself. How am I ever going to follow you?"

I was so overwhelmed I did not realize until she walked away that it was Portia di Rossi herself. It was a truly magical night that left me speechless, which nothing ever does.

That night also led to the Human Rights Campaign putting me on a tour around the country, where I spoke at a variety of galas in different cities. I will not lie—it was some of the most fun I've ever had. I felt like a mini-celebrity, and for a couple of months, it was a real blast. Eventually, I even made my way to the HRC National Dinner, their largest fundraising gala that about 3,000 people attend. If I thought it was cool and nerve-racking to speak after Senator Barbara Boxer, try this one on for size: I was told that I would be speaking after President Obama, who was currently in office. I could not fathom something of this proportion at my then eighteen years of age.

The night before the National Dinner, I went to a meet-and-greet where I knew I would have the chance to meet President Obama. As he entered the small library where the lucky fifty or so of us were packed in, a hush came over the room. He exuded confidence, grace, and charisma like nothing I had ever seen. He gave a short speech about how passionately he believed in our cause and how he was dedicated to helping us advance the LGBTQ agenda, and then he started making his rounds. Watching him walk up to me, I think I had a near-out-of-body experience. He introduced himself (as if I didn't know who he was) and shook my hand. I told him I would be speaking after him the next night and how nervous I was.

He chuckled and said, "Don't worry, Chelsea, I'll just be your warm-up act."

I was so comfortable talking to one of the most powerful figures in the world; it was shocking. Without even thinking twice, I actually put my hand on his arm at one point since it felt natural. It was just such a joy to talk to him, like talking to an old friend.

The next night, I was waiting backstage at the convention center before my turn to speak. I was less nervous at this point, thank goodness. All of a sudden, in came this massive cloud of Secret Service. I am not kidding—probably fifteen people surrounded the president as he entered the premises, and as if that weren't enough, there were massive army-type men with huge weapons at every entrance. The group suddenly came to a halt (seamlessly, I might add) about twenty-five feet from where I was standing. Everyone started to look at one another, confused, and then out of the crowd came Mr. President himself. We were all still trying to figure out what was going on when he walked right up to me.

He took my hand and said, "Hi, Chelsea, good to see you again. I am so proud of all the work you're doing."

I have no idea what I said. I think I managed to squeak out a "Thank-you" as I picked my jaw up off the ground. I know I was definitely staring. He glided back to his protectors and continued the move onto stage right where he was to make his entrance.

The woman standing next to me leaned over and said, "Oh my God, he remembered you," and started crying. I continued to stand there in shock. I think I may have cried, and then I may have been told by someone to stop because I would mess up my makeup. It was the most surreal thing that had ever happened to me.

I have continued to this day to do my best to make a difference in the LGBTQ+ community and to learn from them and other underrepresented communities across the country. It is one of the greatest joys in the world to feel like you're making a difference. I'm so grateful that HRC allowed me the opportunity to realize a dream and ignite a passion for love and giving in my heart, and I strive (and sometimes fail) to live by Booker T. Washington's words, "Those who are happiest are those who do the most for others."

ⓖ ⓖ ⓖ

Something that stuck with me after my encounter with the one of the most powerful leaders in the world was this: If the president can remember my name (whether or not he had to ask someone what it was before he came up to me), we can all do a better job of remembering people's names and what they tell us. When he remembered my name, I felt so overwhelmingly special. It feels like that person is listening and they care enough to remember. We don't remember people's names when we're thinking too much about what we are going to say while they're telling us about themselves. If we don't really focus and remain present, then we are not truly there with that person, working our hardest to learn about their life and their story. We are too fixated on us and our story. It is a choice to focus on yourself rather than someone else when they are speaking to you. Since this encounter, when I realized truly how much hearing your name can mean, I have worked really hard to remember people's names and find ways to help myself along the way. We can put them in our phones in the notes section just in case we know we forget easily. We can text ourselves. We can also write down a little bit about what people say to us. We can do our part to make others feel special. We can do our part to try to make others feel the way the president made me feel. Life gives us so many tiny ways to make people feel special—easy tricks, really. It takes two seconds and makes a world of difference.

◎ ◎ ◎

What are some ways you can brainstorm that might make other people feel special? And while you're at it, what are some things you can do to make yourself feel special?

CHAPTER 15

I THINK WE MAY NEED TO DO A LITTLE RE-EVALUATION

"You gain strength, courage, and confidence by every experience in which you really stop to look fear in the face. Do the thing you think you cannot do."

—Eleanor Roosevelt

I remember back in junior year of high school when I was suddenly struck by the notion that I had to find a college where I wanted to go and where they wanted me as much as I wanted them. The day I sat down to start my college applications was one I will never forget. I sat in the library of my high school with a bunch of other high school seniors and stared at the common application. It asked for my mother's information and my father's information. Before I'd tried to prove anything about my worth, there was already a speed bump. I really did not know what to do. There was no room on that standardized form for a situation that wasn't so standard. I had been listening to my teachers for years, saying, "Go tell your mom this or that," and always muttering under my breath, "Or dad..." and for some reason that day, it really got under my skin. It didn't seem fair. I called my college counselor over and asked, "What do I do?"

She said patiently, "Just put down your Dad under the mother category and your Daddy under the father one."

I looked at her for a minute and then thought it was time to say what was on my mind, "But he's not my mom and I don't think he'd appreciate being labeled like that."

My college counselor sat down next to me. "It's no big deal, sweetie, it's just a label. They'll be able to figure it out, and I really don't think your Dad will mind."

I wanted to apply to college, after all, so I just forced myself to type in the information like she told me to, but it felt wrong. It felt like a lie. It was not the truth about our family and we did not fit into their little box of what a family was supposed to look like, and it made me mad. When I was at home living my life with my dads, I never felt different, but out in the world on a daily basis, I felt excluded just by the little things people would say. I was never bullied because I had two gay dads, but I always felt like I sat a bit to the left of normal. I always had to explain myself and I was always labeled: "Oh, that's the girl who has two gay dads." And while sometimes it made me cool and set me apart, I always felt like it was the shadow that followed me. I was not the girl who was the really good dancer or the smart kid who got a lot of A's. I was the girl with two gay dads. On the one hand, I wanted to stand up and fight for families like mine. On the other hand, I wanted to be able to fill out a simple form without being reminded of having a different label and box for my family every step of the way, especially at a time when I just really wanted to fit in.

My dads didn't make me feel different and neither did my friends, but society as a whole put me on the outside. I was the example, sometimes for better, sometimes for worse. I had a label and an identity that had nothing to do with me. I was categorized based on the family I was born into and not because of the unique attributes I bring to the world as a human, so I learned to play it up. I learned to make having gay dads my thing. I wore it like a badge, and I milked it for all it was worth. It became the subject of my college essay. It was the butt of all my jokes. I decided that instead of pushing against a label that did not really define me, but rather my parentage, I could use it as a platform, as a steppingstone to make myself memorable in a world where everyone wants to be the same. It was also a way, I saw, to change hearts and minds. It was an amazing advantage, but it has also made my parents so much a part of how I define myself. As an adult I started thinking it was the only interesting thing about me.

There is no "me" without a discussion about my parents, which is weird, because I am a separate human being with a fascinating life that is more than just where I came from. I forget that a lot. I've also realized I'm not the only one categorized by their family history and where they came from. We categorize everyone we meet. We want to know their story, check them out, make sure they fit our idea of what is popular, pretty, or perfect. Putting people in boxes is a societal thing. We all do it. We all try to put ourselves in boxes, to make ourselves fit...even maybe where we don't. I eventually came to the conclusion that my box has wavy lines and fuzzy edges, and I started thinking that everyone else's does, too, even the seemingly perfect people. We are all a little blurry. We are all a constellation of our experiences, and we deserve to share every facet of our being that we choose with the world, to help us find our people—the ones whose constellations bring us joy, beauty, and light. We are more than where we came from, although where we come from has shaped much of who we are, and that's an incredible thing; but, back to the horrifying adventure that is applying to college.

I was applying for Bachelor of Fine Arts Musical Theater programs, which are all ridiculously hard to get into. But the whole process, to be honest, is stressful and depressing. As if applying to college, trying to get good grades, taking the SAT, and making yourself a well-rounded young human is not enough, they want you to prepare "Broadway ready" auditions on top of all of that. The year that I applied, in most BFA musical theater programs, there were about twenty spots available and thousands of people auditioning. It was an intense year is the understatement of the decade.

Colleges are so fascinating to me. Some of the most popular universities are in the middle of these tiny towns that are predominantly populated by college students, faculty, and staff, and there's probably just one or two hotels to host visiting families. If you live in a college town, you are bombarded by students who have mistaken the actual town for a part of the campus and proceeded to take it over in its entirety.

I was obsessed with one such university in one of these minuscule towns. To me, this school was the be-all and end-all, the place I wanted to go more than anything ever in the whole entire world. It was the Hogwarts of BFA musical theater programs. I was desperate to go to a big university with tons of school spirit. I wanted something totally opposite from where I had spent my somewhat torturous high school years (and I had it better than most). Not only did this university have a spectacular BFA program, but it also had some of the things my high school did not—like boys, and school spirit.

Dad and I checked in at the local Sheraton, receiving the normal strange looks at the reception desk when we said we were staying in the same room, a room with only one bed. We tended to have to explain ourselves, unlike the typical mother/daughter or father/son pairs, to the shocked-looking hotel employees who thought I must either be the youngest gold digger in the world or Dad the creepiest man alive... or both. This time Dad had been upgraded to a suite, though, so that was cool.

As we were going to sleep that night, I was already talking non-stop about the next day with an overwhelming amount of nerves and excitement. This was it! The day I was going to see the school of my dreams. The more I thought about it, the more nervous and stressed I got. After Dad realized there would be no calming me down, he suggested we turn on the TV and see if maybe *Friends* was on. If you know me, you know the quickest way to calm me down and shut me up is to turn on *Friends*. Preferably "The One Where Ross Is Fine" or "The One with All the Football." As soon as we turned on the TV, a headline popped up: BREAKING NEWS, FLUFFY THE CAT IS DEAD. The local news channel proceeded to go on and on about the local feline, Fluffy, who had gone missing the week prior, and had now turned up dead.

I burst into tears... tears of astonishment and hilarity. I could not stop laughing. I mean, I'm sure Fluffy was a great cat, and I was very sorry for his owners who had to endure this terrible loss, but I had never seen local news focus on something that seemed so trivial. In LA, horrific as it is, most homicides don't even make the news unless it's egregiously heinous or it's the death of a celebrity. I was so shocked by this small-town news report, and it truly warmed my heart. I thought any town where Fluffy the Cat's death was a headline couldn't be all that scary or intimidating. I had been so unbearably nervous to tour this school, and for some reason Fluffy the Cat gave me the comfort to know I could manage anything that came my way. So, thanks Fluff—if you're up in kitty heaven wondering if your life had meaning, I want you to know you gave me great comfort, support, and a good laugh in a moment of need, and I am forever grateful. The tour the next day was spectacular and left me even more in love with the school than I was before: stunning campus, gorgeous buildings, spectacular program. Watching a show that was currently running on campus, I stared at the stage, envisioning myself up there. I had a good feeling that this place would become my home. Regardless of how far away it was from my family, or how snowy it might be, I would do anything to be a part of this program.

A few weeks later, I auditioned for the school. I performed my comedic monologue and left the audience of one laughing hysterically. I even saw the pianist nod as I sang my thirty-two bars of the audition song I had chosen. I was feeling pretty good. Then after all of this preamble, I just had to wait. For months. My fate was totally in the hands of people I did not know, and I just hoped and dreamed and prayed. I felt a connection with this school. It was the best school I had ever seen in my whole life. It was the perfect fit, and I knew the Universe was going to take care of me.

Every day after school, I would check my email, awaiting a college acceptance. One day I got in Dad's car on my way home from school and saw the email. It seemed to take an eternity to load and when finally I saw "We're sorry to inform you . . ." I didn't have to read any more. I felt completely deflated. They had not even put me on their waitlist. Being onstage and performing in musical theater had been my dream since forever—how could they not understand that? And much, much worse, it made me think: *Am I actually not as talented as I thought I was?* I leaned my head against the headrest, just willing myself to get home and away from people. Dad did his best to console me, but I don't think I heard a word. I didn't want to run into any of my friends who may have been just accepted into this elite program because that would just be the worst. (Spoiler alert: One of my friends did end up getting accepted and attending that very program.)

When we got home, Dad checked the mail as he always did, and there was a letter from my other top-choice school! We were so relieved, thinking, okay today will not be all bad, it could be really amazing. We would finally know where I'd be spending the next four years of my life! He handed me the letter, and I opened it as quickly as I could, feeling my stomach tighten. Instead of the pristine stationery welcoming me to the beautiful campus, it was another rejection—the perfect cherry on top of this bitter college rejection sundae. I felt beaten. This could not be happening. I ran to my room, collapsed on the floor, and cried and cried and cried. I thought the feeling of rejection might swallow me up. Dad stood in the doorway as I wailed, "What is wrong with me? Why do they not want me?"

I did the only thing I knew how to do: I put on my leotard and tights and got ready for dance class. I was one of the most dedicated dancers my age at my studio. I danced seven days a week for hours, and for my vocal training, I trained at the most elite music school in Los Angeles. I even drove an hour and a half to take Latin Ballroom lessons. My parents had hired special acting coaches to get my monologues prepared for these auditions. There was no way I could have trained more or better. It just was what it was. I went to class, told my dance family what had happened, and got hugs all around. They were outraged that I had not been accepted, and that was all I needed to hear because these friends were the people who really knew me and my talent, and I trusted them with my heart more than I ever would a stupid school with a great reputation.

That day became known as Black Friday in my family, and as if Black Friday was not enough, the rejections kept coming, each one like a dagger to my pride. I was even getting rejected from schools I'd thought were my safety schools. At one point I realized I only had two more schools to hear from. One was ranked the top BFA musical theater program in the country and another was a small liberal arts college in rural Pennsylvania. It was like the agony and the ecstasy. I was pretty sure I could write off the best program in the country when every other BFA school I applied to had already rejected me. The funny thing was that when I visited the program ranked number one for musical theater in the country, I did not like the school. I didn't think the people were nice and when the tour guide said, "If you get into this program, you don't turn us down," I thought that, no matter what, I would turn these people down if they were so arrogant as to think we could not do better. As it became my last option, though, I didn't know what I'd do. The letter from the small liberal arts college came. I'd been accepted with a sizeable scholarship, and I all but threw it in the trash. I did not want to go there. I wanted something else— liberal arts was not what I had signed up for. I had become so fixated with the idea that I *had* to attend a bachelor of fine arts program that to me liberal arts felt *less than*. I was competitive with many of the girls I went to school with and most of my close friends were also applying, and getting accepted to, BFA programs. The label, Bachelor of Fine Arts, felt important to a young triple-threat like me, and truthfully I didn't have a great understanding of what a liberal arts education meant as I had spent so much time focusing on the BFA programs.

Then the letter came from the top BFA musical theater program in the country. Out of all the schools I had applied to, this one had priority waitlisted me. They only accepted fifteen people out of the thousands who applied and should one of those fifteen not want their spot, I would be one of the first people to gain acceptance. The only catch was that I had to guarantee I would go there before they would consider taking me off the waitlist.

I sat in the kitchen for what felt like hours with the two letters staring at me, and my parents staring at me staring at the letters. I just wanted to decide. I did not want to wait any longer. I wanted to know where I would be living, what I would be studying, and everything else that comes along with college life. But I could not make a snap decision about something so big, no matter how much I wanted to. Spring break was approaching and I decided to take the time to think and think I did. Ten days later, I sat down at the kitchen island again, the same place I'd sat days before, my parents standing exactly as they had been, trying to casually make conversation. In my heart, I knew what I wanted. I was just fighting the battle of what everyone else would think, but with a decision as massive as this one, I knew I had to listen to my heart and not care about the *mishegas* (meaning "crazy stuff" in Yiddish), as my grandpa would say.

I finally looked up and told my dads, "I want to go where I'm wanted. This school is offering me a scholarship, and as much as I want a BFA, everyone was so nice at the other school. The campus was really pretty, and as much as I hate to give up the dream of getting into one of those BFA programs, I think this is where I want to go."

Both of my parents exhaled, they were so relieved. It was exactly what they wanted for me, too, even though they would have supported me no matter what my decision was. At the end of the day, who does not want to be where they are wanted as opposed to being at the bottom of the barrel, just hoping to be noticed?

It was one of the best decisions I ever made. The people at Muhlenberg College—which became my alma mater—were kind, they were my family, and guess what? I still graduated with a degree in theater and dance from one of the top bachelor of arts programs in the country, and I got to perform more than I ever would have at any of those other schools. I became Muhlenberg's biggest advocate. I was a tour guide. I even stayed summers there to perform between semesters, and I got a fantastic education to boot. I also met the people who became some of my very best friends in the entire world. We all want what is exclusive and elusive, we all want what we can't have, but sometimes by taking what you can have, you end up with something more magical than you would've ever thought was possible.

ⓖ ⓖ ⓖ

My friend, after this experience, I started looking at rejection as my light-up game show arrow. Every time something didn't work out, while I may have been deeply disappointed in the moment, I saw my arrow pointing to something much more meant for me. My college counselor once said, "College admissions are a match to be made, not a prize to be won." At the time I completely dismissed it. Now, looking back, I see how valuable her words were. We can be so obsessed with competing with our peers, looking for perfect instead of perfect for us, and we stop ourselves from actually choosing the place/person/thing that's best for us. This idea can be applied to everything we do in life. I have faced rejections many, many times since I applied to colleges. In my love life, after being rejected I was ultimately led to the exact person I was meant to be with (more on that later). And in my work it brought me here, writing this book and even then, I watched publisher after publisher reject my manuscript. Ultimately, in both situations I ended up exactly where I needed to be and where I really wanted to be, but my perception of what I thought I wanted would sometimes lead to disappointment in the process. However, following that light-up game show arrow of rejection has never led me astray and it can do the same for you. Rejection is not a wall placed on your path, but an arrow nudging you (no matter how painfully) in the direction of what is meant for you. What is meant for you is magical in its own way. So, after you face rejection, take your time to feel all the feelings that come along with it. Give yourself a minute to go back to your gratitude, do something fun, and take a breather, and then get back up on that horse because magic awaits.

What if we were to choose what honestly felt best for us in our hearts and flip rejections on their head as pathways instead of blockages? What would it be like to go back and reevaluate your rejections; what magic might you see then?

CHAPTER 16

NOTHING IS BLACK AND WHITE

"Life is like riding a bicycle.
To keep your balance, you must keep moving."
—**Albert Einstein**

I t all started with the whispering. When I walked into a room it would stop and an eerie hush would fall between Dad and Daddy. They would stop talking, but they would not stop staring at each other. They were obviously concerned about something I wasn't supposed to know about. My parents have always shared everything with me. I mean, like, way too much. We are a family of oversharers, so I knew something was very much off. I also knew better than to ask what it was. I was seventeen when we went to visit some friends in Maine, and my parents finally had to come clean to me.

When I was two years old, Daddy, the genius accountant, met a couple, Mike and Stacey, at a dear friend's birthday party. Mike and

Stacey were both born and raised in Hawaii. Mike owned several car dealerships across the Hawaiian islands and was known, unbeknownst to my family, as quite the Hawaiian cowboy. Stacey was a descendant of a European sailor who landed on the islands in the 1800s and stayed and built a fortune. Stacey was one of the beneficiaries to the trust her European ancestor had created, which was easily worth over five billion dollars. Mike and Stacey were Hawaiian heavy hitters to say the least.

At the birthday party that night, Mike mentioned that he was looking for a new accountant and swiftly Daddy offered up his services. Both Stacey and Mike had taken an instant liking to Daddy and without another thought they agreed to hire him to do their accounting. By the next morning, boxes of their tax documents were showing up at Daddy's office so he could begin his work. For over a decade, other members of Stacey's and Mike's families also grew to know my Daddy, and eventually he became the accountant to hundreds of clients on the islands and a trusted advisor to the majority of the trust's beneficiaries. He traveled to Hawaii four times a year, almost always with Dad and me in tow, and we became closer and closer to Daddy's clients there. They welcomed us into their homes and considered us family. They even asked me to call them Auntie Stacey and Uncle Mike. After many years, Mike retired from running the dealerships and his son, Randy, took over the day-to-day operations. Randy was not a good guy by pretty much anyone's definition. He was slimy and certainly not aboveboard with many of his business dealings, always having his own interests at the forefront of his mind. And his father was, after all, a rough and tumble cowboy who believed he was entitled to do as he pleased.

Mike owned thousands of acres in Kauai. You could literally get lost walking around some of his properties, they were so massive. I grew up wandering the orange groves on one of them, picking oranges and eating them in the shade of the trees, away from the hot Hawaiian sun, while Daddy met for hours with Mike on the veranda of his expansive plantation-style home.

On one of his properties there was a reservoir that the State of Hawaii was supposed to maintain but never quite got around to. The state claimed Mike had illegally graded the land around the reservoir and covered a spillway, but Mike denied it vehemently. I could not tell you whether or not he had graded illegally. I do not and will never know the truth about that. However, during a terrible storm and the worst rain in over one hundred years, the reservoir's dam gave way and flooded the valley below, wiping out several homes and killing seven people. From that moment on, everyone who lived on the island knew Mike's name, and the state saw him as public enemy number one. The government kicked into high gear and went on a mission to take Mike down. However, they were having a difficult time proving that Mike actually did illegally grade his land and that the failure of the dam was his fault. So, when they were unsuccessful in convicting him of this, they decided to go after all of his business dealings and companies under the assumption that the grading was not the only illegal activity that Mike had engaged in.

Here is where it starts to involve my family, and please hang in there... there's going to be a lot of business lingo, but if I had to live through it, I swear you can endure a few pages. (Plus, I added footnotes for clarification—you're welcome.)

During the investigation of Mike's businesses, Daddy was the accountant for all of his holdings, both business and personal, and he did Randy's personal tax return, but not the tax returns for the auto dealerships that were now Randy's companies. Unbeknownst to Daddy, Randy and the former accountant for the car dealerships had been illegally deducting personal expenses on the dealerships' tax returns. Eventually these dealings came to Daddy's attention and he told them, in writing, that they should stop deducting these expenses immediately. Perhaps naïvely, Daddy believed they would stop the illegal activity without ever verifying for himself whether they did or not. When he filed Randy's personal return, he took the numbers the dealership's accountant and personal CPA had given him at face value.

While all of these state investigations were happening, Mike sold a building that had been acquired in a 1031 exchange.[1] If Daddy had reported this transaction on Mike's tax return correctly, it would have cost him over one million dollars in taxes, which Mike did not have the money for at the time. Daddy took pity on Mike as a long-time client, an elderly man, and a friend, knowing all that Mike had been through, and decided not to declare the entire gain made through the 1031 on Mike's return. That saved Mike from having to pay the tax.

Remember, Mike is someone the state and federal governments *really* want to take down. Randy is committing fraud through his business and both Mike and Randy are being investigated, which Daddy had knowledge of when he chose not to report this 1031 exchange gain on Mike's personal tax return. It does not take a brain surgeon to figure out that eventually Daddy was going to be investigated. Ultimately, there were two charges that the federal government made against Daddy: conspiracy to defraud the Internal Revenue

---

[1] A 1031 exchange allows you to exchange one property for another like-kind property and also allows you to defer the payment of the capital gains tax you would otherwise have to pay to the federal government. Please see the Internal Revenue Code for a much more in-depth and detailed explanation of what this is and how this works. Do not take my word for it.

Service and assisting in the filing of a false federal income tax return. In addition to these two charges, they made many untrue charges and were intent on taking Daddy down because of his association with this family. The government pressured all parties involved to get a conviction and, as part of this, convinced Mike's former accountant to lie and tell the judge that he had sent Daddy hundreds of documents explaining previous transactions. Daddy had never seen any of those documents; however, it was the former accountant's word against his.

At that point there was an assumed paper trail, which would be hard to prove was never actually sent. Daddy also had committed fraud by not declaring the entire 1031 exchange gain on Mike's personal tax return, so our lawyers told him the best thing he could do would be to take a plea deal and cooperate against Mike to lessen his sentence. Take the plea deal he did, cooperate against Mike he did not. Daddy is loyal to those he cares about to a fault and felt he had already made a grave enough mistake by not reporting the full 1031 exchange gain; he would not also lie and tell the judge that Mike had asked him to alter the return. The prosecutors pressured Daddy to lie on the witness stand, which he did not, and Mike was found, in this instance, rightfully innocent.

When they first started investigating Daddy, he told Dad not to worry, that nothing had been done out of the ordinary and it would all be okay. I was, at that point, blissfully unaware. The years of the investigation wore on and intensified and then Daddy was forced to admit that he did not know what the outcome would be and that he had made a grave, grave mistake. He also learned that under normal circumstances something like what he did on this tax return, when found by the government, would result in an audit assessment and the client would end up paying the tax, interest, and perhaps a financial penalty—but nothing more. However, nothing about this situation seemed "normal" anymore. My parents hunkered down and supported each other as each day the future looked more and more bleak. It was when Daddy was indicted on those two charges that my parents told me what was going on.

I sat on the bed in the unfamiliar hotel room and cried. Daddy is my hero, the kindest, most caring man I know. His clients feel uplifted when they leave his office, which I believe is not so common when it comes to accountants. The guy who used to arrange blueberries into a smiley face on my oatmeal every morning. The person who taught me what unconditional love is. It did not add up. It was like I had been told all my life that one plus one equals two, but now somehow it equaled three. The lawyers attempted to assuage my fears. They promised he would only be put on probation for a few years and then our lives would go back to normal, especially since he did not have a criminal record. They said the absolute worst-case scenario would be that he would have to spend three months in prison. Daddy and the word *prison* in the same sentence seemed unimaginable to me. I put the thought out of my mind and told myself that he would get a slap on the wrist, maybe pay a fine, *maybe* be put on probation, and that would be that. It would be a year and a half from the time he pled guilty until the sentencing. So, we picked up and kept moving because what the hell else are you supposed to do? Daddy did a bad thing, he made a major irreversible mistake, but he was still one of the most incredible people I knew.

One thing I forgot to mention. The prosecutor told Daddy that if he did not plead guilty then I, his daughter, could kiss my college degree goodbye. He explained that the prosecution would make sure I was put on the stand in Hawaii to testify every single week of my college career, regardless of the fact that I had known nothing about what was going on. The prosecution said that by the time I was done, I would have spent so many months, and maybe years, away from my school in Pennsylvania that I would never get my degree. Daddy wanted to protect me and so he pled guilty. His determination to protect me and love for me never ceases to amaze me.

This process was the first time I had come into contact with this kind of injustice, or justice, or whatever you want to call it, firsthand. In the past, when I had seen people on the news convicted of a crime go to jail, I assumed they were bad people who had done something horrible, and they deserved the punishment. I will never again automatically judge someone that way. The law may be black and white, but people's lives and minds are not. I heard what people said about Daddy behind his back and to his face. The way the people in Hawaii who used to be his friends started vilifying him and spreading lies about his character—it was horrific. Poor Daddy was so horrified that he had gotten our family into this mess that I was terrified he would never forgive himself. All we could do was breathe, wait, and keep moving because sometimes life doesn't give you another option.

© © ©

When you are staring down the barrel of a potentially life-altering gun and you have no control, it can be terrifying. We want to know the outcome. We want to have surety. We want to skip to the last chapter before it has even been written. We have very little control over so many variables that affect our lives. Truly the only thing we can always control is ourselves and our reactions to events. In the time we were waiting to see what my Daddy's fate would be, I had an opportunity. I could sit and stress and wonder what might happen, or I could rest in the comfort of knowing I could handle anything that came my way someway, somehow. I'm here to tell you that you have that power, too. You can control your reactions to events, and you can handle anything that comes your way. Really, you can. You are built for your life and you can make anything you want out of it. Sometimes during the process of living, life will feel really hard, and those "less favorable" emotions will come up and that is absolutely normal. It's okay to be a whole human having a full human experience. Let yourself feel and process but know there are always multiple interpretations to every situation. Just ask my parents any time they have a disagreement—there's Daddy's side, Dad's side, and then what actually happened. None of us own the capital "T" truth, we are just the owners of our perspectives, and we might as well choose a perspective that makes us feel good as often as possible.

ⓖ ⓖ ⓖ

What's something that has happened to you recently that you wish had a different outcome? What is a different perspective you could have about that same occurrence? How does this new perspective make you feel?

CHAPTER 17

WHAT'S NEW AND SHINY AND TERRIFIED ALL OVER?

"The fears we don't face become our limits."

—Robin Sharma

I hate when people say the only constant thing in life is change. I hate it mostly because it's true. I love a touch of spontaneity, but just a touch. I like to feel safe and to know what I should be wearing. Any time any kind of change occurs in my life, be it massive or minuscule, I have what my family likes to call an adjustment period. I am essentially a creature of habit, and if I'm asked to change something in my life or something in my life starts to change by itself, I really need some time to adapt. It usually involves a good cry, a cup of tea, and some big hugs, and then I am prepared to make the change or to let life change around me.

My Auntie Melanie once said my mind is like a New Mexico sky. One minute it is stunning and the clouds are puffy and gorgeous—the next minute a thunderstorm blows in, destroying everything in its path, rain tormenting the villagers and soaking the desert landscape. But then, five minutes later, the sky is beautiful again, sun setting with a purple hue and not a drop of rain to be seen.

I like things a certain way. I like routine. I like my planner and my lists because they, in my mind, "keep me safe." My heart also knows change is exciting: new people and places, new food (one of the best parts), a new perspective. Change is a beautiful and terrifying thing. I think everyone can agree that the unknown of anything is the scariest thing in the world. It is the unknown that scares some people about gay people. They have never met anyone who is gay so they don't know what to expect. I think they worry that if they become okay with gay, lesbian, bisexual, transgender, gender nonconforming, or queer individuals, then that will change their fundamental belief system, which is a massive paradigm shift that scares the utter crap out of people. I am a firm believer in making unknown things into known things so that life feels less scary, because I prefer a not scary life to a scary life.

One of the things I always knew I was going to have to change in my life was my fear of being away from my parents. I have had insane separation anxiety from my parents since I was a little girl. I hated not being with them all the time, even for an hour at dance class. If I couldn't see them in the window outside of the dance studio, I would lose my mind. This anxiety of mine persisted until late into my teenage years—something I'm not so keen on admitting. It evolved as I grew up. I wasn't afraid of being away from my parents by the time I was a teenager, but I was afraid of being in situations where I was misunderstood without them by my side. So when it came time to apply for colleges, everyone was pretty much dumbfounded that I only applied to schools 3,000 or more miles away from home. I knew if I was going to be independent, I had to go far away or I was never going to fly out of the nest. I had to change my surroundings, meet all new people, and leap into the great unknown in a major way. My parents told me they were so proud that I had decided to make this move, even though I know Daddy cried every night at the thought of me living so far away. When I chose Muhlenberg College, a school in Allentown, Pennsylvania, it became real. I was really going to make the move. I would be a five-and-a-half-hour plane ride from home at a minimum. I knew it was what I wanted and once I decided I was going to do it, it would have been pretty much impossible to change my mind. I am a bit relentless as they say... and not so great at admitting defeat.

It was hands-down one of the best decisions I ever made, but it did not feel like that at the start. I remember flying in for accepted students' day and thinking, *Oh my God, what have I done?* My parents were going to drop me off in a few months' time in a random city in Pennsylvania—a city that people have only heard of from the Billy Joel song—where I knew no one and would be living with a stranger. I was insane, I'd lost my mind, someone turn this plane around.

We landed and drove to the bed and breakfast in the middle of nowhere that my parents had booked without knowing anything about the place. Mistake number one. Dad and I went to the front desk while Daddy sat in the car attending to his emails. Dad proudly told the hotel staff that I would be attending Muhlenberg College and that I wanted to explore Allentown.

The lady at the front desk looked at my Dad and said, "Really? Allentown? Ugh, I don't even think there's anything there."

I took one look at Dad, started to cry, and ran for the car. Daddy, still knee-deep in emails, was startled by my sudden entrance.

"They (sharp intake of breath) said (choking sob) there's (ridiculously loud sniffling) nothing (hiccup) there," I said, through a waterfall of tears.

Daddy was crushed that I was so sad, and luckily Dad returned before Daddy started crying, too.

Dad said, "Let's just go and explore! That lady doesn't know what she's talking about anyway!"

He sounded very confident, but I could tell behind all of that confidence that he was willing himself to be right. We started to drive through the beautiful fields of rural Pennsylvania, my panic slowly subsiding. At every turn, I was looking out the window in hopes of finding some semblance of civilization.

Finally, after what felt like an eternity, we came upon a suburban strip mall right near my soon-to-be college. Low and behold what was there but an Outback Steakhouse! Never in my life have I been so happy to see a Bloomin' Onion! It was something I knew and something I could relate to—if there was an Outback, then there must be civilization. It's so funny how your mind does that to you. The second you find a touch point, everything turns around. It's all going to be okay and just because of some mediocre steaks. Needless to say, I was relieved.

Two months later, I was back in Allentown, and it was time to move into the dorms. The day before move-in we received an email from the school that freshman parents would have to leave after lunch on move-in day. Dad, Daddy, and I stared at each other in disbelief. We were supposed to have two more days together. They were supposed to stay, help me unpack, and spend time with me before they flew back to California. We were supposed to have more time. We *definitely* were supposed to have more time! I immediately emailed my new advisor to make sure this was not a mistake. I mean, after all, this was college and I was supposed to be an adult, so why did they get to tell me when my parents had to leave? We found out that it was true and there were no *ifs*, *ands*, or *buts* about this rule. I had a little meltdown, but afterward I was okay, though Daddy definitely was not. This new world was going to be my new home and I was determined to make the best of whatever was offered to me.

As we approached campus, the orientation team pointed out the queue of cars headed for Prosser Hall, my new home, which had all the charm of a penitentiary. Once we reached the front of the line, a very well-meaning upperclassman greeted our rental car, filled to the brim with every worldly possession I could cram in, and directed me to my room. Then a group of upperclassmen descended upon our car and helped us carry all of my things—there were a lot of things. We were highly impressed with the organization of it all. We filled up my room until it was perfect, with shabby chic pillows and even a tiny chandelier that hung over my desk, below my lofted bed. We were almost done setting up by the time my roommate got there, and I think she was a bit overwhelmed by what she saw when she entered the room. Two gay men and their daughter, making a bed with specially ordered shabby chic sheets and assembling extra storage for my abundance of clothes. We were a walking stereotype. She was kind, albeit shocked, as was her family. She was a good Christian girl from New Jersey, and she welcomed me with mostly open arms.

After everything had found its place, we realized it was time for lunch. We knew what was coming as soon as we were done eating, so we all ate slower than normal, trying to delay the inevitable. When the bell tolled, signaling it was time for the first meeting with advisory groups, we had pits in our stomachs. My parents walked me to where I would be meeting with my fellow honors program students (yes, I am a nerd), and we looked at each other with tears in our eyes. I hugged them once, then one more time for good luck. Out of nowhere, it seemed, this incredibly tall, sweet angel came to my rescue. He introduced himself as Eric, and we discovered that he was in the same honors program I was. He saw that the three of us were struggling with our goodbyes and in his infinite wisdom told me I just had to rip the Band-Aid off. So with one more hug for each of my dads, I turned around and walked with Eric into the nearest building. I did not dare look back because I thought I might implode from how much I already missed my dads. No one had ever dared to separate us like this before, and this was somehow my idea. However, as soon as I was sitting awkwardly among strangers who all were also feeling all the feelings of the day, I felt like I was going to be okay.

I called my parents the next day and told them I'd already made a group of girlfriends. We ate all of our meals together and saw each other every single second we were not in class. We started a group text we embarrassingly named "The Sexy Seven." I remember lying in my bed, which had been lofted so high it almost touched the ceiling, telling my dads all about how exciting the first day was, and thinking, *Yep, I am going to like it here.* And four of the most incredible years of my life ensued. It was my perfect school! The small, beautiful campus attracted the most wonderful students, as well as professors and advisors. I was truly encompassed in my new home.

ⓖ ⓖ ⓖ

My friend, the unknown is always the scariest, but the cool thing about the unknown is that once you do the unknown thing, it becomes a known thing, and the more unknown things you can turn into known things, the less scary and bigger your world is. I literally have hated the unknown for so much of my life. Even trying a new restaurant freaked me out. I realized that a lot of my fear of the unknown was also a fear of looking or sounding stupid and embarrassing myself or a fear that I might not fit in or not look like I was "in the know." Do you know that feeling, too? Our fear can sometimes stop us from living life. Every time I would try a new restaurant, my palms would sweat because I was afraid I wouldn't know where to find the bathroom, or I wouldn't know where to check in for our reservation. It seems so silly, but it was so real for me. It's okay if the unknown is scary, friend. But, as you keep finding these unknown things and embracing change, your life just gets bigger and more exciting. The second you put a wall up to change, you also start to wall yourself in, and before you know it, you're in a box and afraid to do anything new. Start reminding yourself every time your heart races and your hands get clammy when you're doing something new that you have done many new things before and will do many more to come and look at it as something exciting instead of petrifying. We're all newbies sometimes and sometimes you're just going to have to look like one and that is a-okay.

© © ©

When has change served you? How can you remember those moments where change has been a positive force in your life as a means of moving forward when you are feeling afraid?

CHAPTER 18

NO, YOU MAY NOT HAVE A BITE OF MY FRIENDSHIP PIE

"Friendship is born at that moment when
one person says to another, what, you too?
I thought I was the only one."

—C. S. Lewis

During my freshman year of college, I met an amazing woman named Danni. She was one of the funniest people I knew, and we connected instantly. Neither of us really got along with our respective roommates, and we lived on the same floor so we spent pretty much all of our time together. She sat in my pink butterfly chair while I sat on my desk chair that leaned back so far I almost fell off it every five minutes, until finally, after we had exhausted every possible avenue of conversation, I would roll into bed and Danni would walk down the hall back to her room at two in the morning. She was one of a handful of friends I had who were not in the theater and dance department. Oftentimes it was a relief to get away from all the drama the theater department inherently and ironically contained.

At the end of freshman year, it came time to choose your roommate for sophomore year. Danni and I did not even have to talk about what was going to happen. It was a given. Why wouldn't we live together? We spent every night hanging out and talking in my room. How much more convenient it would be if we did the same thing in a room we shared and from our own beds. As it turned out, it was indeed so much more fun living with a roommate I was friends with and also a whole lot more complicated. When I lived with someone I was not very close with, I didn't really expect to get along with her, but when I was living with someone I already loved, I assumed we were only going to grow closer.

Danni did not have a lot of friends, and I had an entire group of people I was always doing shows and rehearsing with. I knew Danni felt lonely. One night, early on in our sophomore year, she came home and said, "Please don't think I'm crazy."

I had no idea where this was going, but I said, "I'm sure whatever it is, I've done something crazier." The next thing that came out of her mouth was shocking to me.

"I think I'm going to rush a sorority."

I wasn't sure what to say so I looked down at my homework as a means of collecting myself, feeling deflated and slightly confused about what this choice was going to mean, knowing I was not someone who had any interest in taking part in a sorority. I think I realized at that moment, whether I wanted to believe it or not, that her decision was a turning point in our friendship.

"I think it'll be fun for you," I finally managed to get out.

I knew it was the right choice for her, no matter how jealous it made me that she would be making new, and probably cooler, friends than me. Well, that is exactly what happened. She rushed a sorority and developed a completely new social circle that I was not a part of at all. She was out partying, hanging out with frat bros, and doing all of the things I had no interest in but was secretly so jealous of.

I was excited when the end of sophomore year rolled around because I would be spending the next semester studying abroad in Italy. I was sure everything would change with some fresh Tuscan air and a lack of sorority sisters around. Our plan was that we would live together again when I got back to campus after my phenomenal semester in Italy. About two weeks before the end of my sophomore year, though, Danni asked if we could sit down and talk. We sat next to each other at Java Joe's amidst the constant chatter that hums nearby any college coffee stand.

"Chels," she started, and I immediately knew whatever she had to say was not going to be pretty. No one ever starts with your name unless it is something very bad or something extraordinarily good... and I was pretty sure she wasn't proposing to me. I suddenly wished we had opted for a more private place to talk. Danni continued, "I love you so much and you're such an amazing friend, but I think it's best for our friendship if we don't live together when you get back from Italy."

It was like the bottom fell out of my stomach. There was not even time to change her mind.

She went on, "I'm going to live with some of my friends from my sorority."

I urged myself not to cry, even though I felt totally abandoned by my best friend. I was so hurt and so disappointed and I totally should have seen it coming, which made me even more upset. My eyes danced around the top of my latte to-go cup. I fidgeted with the lid, trying to look like I was making sure it was on tight enough as I thought about what I would say. As she listed the reasons she thought it would be better if we didn't live together, I knew it was not her fault alone that we were growing apart. I didn't really want to make it known, though, that I understood things were changing, so all I managed was "I think everything happens for a reason."

It was sad and so hard, but I believed it in my heart to be true, and there was no sense in making her feel bad for changing our plans, even though I so would have loved to make her feel bad at the moment. At the end of the day, it was brave of her to be able to come to me and say what she said, and had she not, she would have resented every minute of us living together and then our friendship would have dissolved completely.

Several months later, when the end of the semester was approaching in Italy, I still needed a place to live. My friend and roommate while I was in Italy, KC, and I were lying in our beds in our bright yellow room in an Italian villa when she mentioned that another friend of ours had two spots open in a campus house, but that there would be a fourth person living there who I didn't know.

I was highly skeptical as I didn't like the idea of getting to know someone by being forced together in a house. "Who would we be living with?" I asked.

"It's Juliette Reilly. She's a year younger than us, but I've been in a show with her. She's quiet but super nice."

KC was always up for something new, and I begrudgingly went along with the plan because I did not know what else to do. I had no other options and figured at least I would have my own room, even if everything else went to hell. As the semester continued in Italy, KC and I struggled with our friendship. It seemed I wasn't destined to live very well with a close friend of mine. KC and I got to a boiling point in our relationship and it started to crumble. It's hard to know what boundaries look like at nineteen, and KC and I didn't have any but were desperately in need of many. As we are both people pleasers and confrontation-averse people, we also refused to talk about the things in our relationship that were upsetting to each other, and instead of communicating and handling them more openly and honestly, we just got more and more angered by each other. We got passive aggressive and shut down. We didn't know how to fix the friendship, but we'd already decided we would live together, so we just kept smiling and ignored the resentment we felt toward each other. It wasn't healthy, but we didn't know any better.

Daddy came back to campus with me that spring to help me move in because I was having a really hard time adjusting to being back after living abroad. Juliette, the new, unknown roommate, happened to be moving into her room, with the help of her dad, at exactly the same time. We exchanged awkward hellos in the hallway outside our rooms. She had also been kicked out of a living situation with people she thought were her best friends, and she felt nearly the same way I did about living with people she didn't already know.

Juliette was really quiet. I mean like super shy. I didn't know what to make of her, but I thought she was cool because she sang and played guitar. One night about a week after moving in together, we all gathered in my room because, thanks to my homosexual parents, it was the best-decorated room to hang out in. We talked for hours and then, one by one, KC and our other roommate, Molly, went to bed. Juliette was sitting in the corner and I asked if she wanted to watch *Friends*. "Sure," she timidly replied.

I turned on my favorite show and about five minutes later, I looked over at that same pink butterfly chair that Danni used to sit in, which was now holding Juliette, and said, "You can come sit on my bed if you want!" I wasn't sure if she would think that was weird or not, but I thought it might be nice to have a new friend, someone who I could feel close with again. It was worth the risk of sounding crazy.

"Sure," she said again, this time slightly more enthusiastic.

She crawled onto my bed next to me, and I can remember sitting there, looking straight at the TV, and thinking, okay, this girl is going to be my best friend. I just had this feeling.

Turns out, I was right. We did everything together, including hiding in our room during hurricanes and snowstorms. Sometimes we would have days-long stakeouts in my room, and we'd play rock paper scissors for who would have to go downstairs and grab the tortilla chips. We would drive around in my car to have a good cry together and go and get McDonald's in the middle of the night because sometimes a Quarter Pounder and Chicken McNuggets are just what you need when boys or friends are acting crazy. It was the first time I felt I had a best friend in my life where it was just easy. Our friendship did not require extra energy—Juliette just got me. We decided to live together again the following year and started searching high and low for new roommates both of us could stand. KC and I had not been able to repair our relationship, so I knew living together wouldn't be healthy for either of us, and our other roommate, Molly, was graduating.

I knew a girl named Alex who was looking for somewhere to live, and Juliette knew someone in her year, Lillian, who also needed to find housing. We convened the potential-new-roommate meeting at our place. First came Lillian. The sweet, blonde, cheerful Vermont girl was all smiles and giggles, one of those people who thinks she's super awkward but is really the least awkward person ever. She took her long dancer legs and folded herself up on the floor. Then Alex arrived. Although I didn't know her all that well, I could already tell I was going to love this girl. There is no other way to describe her other than that she emanates warmth. She *is* the sun, her smile lighting up a room instantaneously. She came into our living room in her oversized Boho-chic sweater, comfy pants, and rain boots, with a cup of tea in hand, just ever so slightly disheveled in that artist kind of way. She did not take herself too seriously, yet she was willing to take seriously whatever anyone else had to say. She was like a cartoon character you just want to hug.

We all sat together awkwardly in our living room to see if we might be compatible. After about five minutes, we decided living with each other would be much better than playing the odds, so live together we would. We were all so different and yet there was always someone in the house who was game for whatever someone else was planning. What was even more wonderful was that we actually made really good roommates. Outside of needing a chore chart to get people to take responsibility for the collective mess we would make, there really wasn't anything to complain about. These women were my people, people who I would stick to for better or for worse.

I made dinner at night and my girls appreciated my taking care of them. Alex would make ridiculously healthy pancakes and kale smoothies, and I would cover everything in butter and lemon pepper to make up for Alex's health food. I taught Juliette to drink way too much coffee, and Lillian and I would rise early whether it was a weekend or not. Lillian even enjoyed shoveling snow—we snagged a good one, folks . . .

Even though we were incredibly different, Lillian being much more devoted to her faith than any of us, Alex being from a bigger, slightly more conservative family, and Juliette being shy and more introspective, we were all connected by being the type of people to stick to our guns and to believe, if not always in ourselves, then in each other. The four of us would sit together in our kitchen talking late into the night, and I would silently think I was right when I told Danni everything happens for a reason. If she hadn't been brave and told me how she felt, I never would have met these girls who changed my life. Five years after graduating college, with thousands of miles separating us, we always manage to stay in each other's lives one way or another. Danni, KC, Jules, Alex, and Lillian have all taught me that I should not be so sad when things do not work out because most times when they don't, there is something totally magical in a brand-new path waiting for me on the other side.

ⓖ ⓖ ⓖ

Sometimes you can go through a really troubling time with a friend, even to the point of not speaking to each other, and come out on the other side loving each other equally, maybe even more, and with boundaries and a better understanding of each other's wants and needs. It can sometimes take time and some distance, but ultimately your friendship has the capacity to be more honest and equitable. It's okay to disagree or to fight, what matters is that you offer up your true and honest self. Sometimes the complete dissolution and then resolution of a relationship is necessary for growth. Sometimes friendships come and go. Such is life. With both KC and Danni, I've found a new form of friendship that works. KC and I even work together. The way our relationship functions now takes into account who we have become and respects what we've gone through in the past. This is an example of what those friendships can be like for you, too. While we may not have been as close throughout the rest of our college careers, we've developed a beautiful friendship post-college, where we can bring our truest selves to the table. It's less exhausting and so much more fun and I believe we all deserve that kind of friendship. To me, that is the only kind of friendship worth having.

ⓒ ⓒ ⓒ

What are some ways you can start to bring your whole self to your relationships? If you feel like you cannot ever be your full self with the people you're surrounded with, what does that mean to you?

CHAPTER 19

THE BURDEN OF VIRGINITY

"The most revolutionary thing a woman
can do is not explain herself."

—Glennon Doyle

I typically pride myself on my discernment when it comes to boys. I didn't stick around if the relationship didn't seem worth my time, or if I got dumped, I tended to get over it pretty quickly. I really am not one to cry over spilled milk, or if I do, it is never for long . . . I wipe up the milk and move on! I never saw much of a point to wallowing in it, and most of the time, I decided those boys were not worth my tears. More than anything, I knew that every time a relationship didn't work out, the Universe was helping me figure out what I did and did not want in a relationship, which would eventually lead me to my perfect person.

The only time it seemed that my system of treating myself with respect failed me was when it came to the desperation with which I wanted to lose my virginity. I know that it should not have been a priority, but somewhere in my soul, I wanted to get past that hurdle and be done. Dad had talked endlessly about how the first time should be special and loving and not a casual quickie, but I felt I just wanted it in the past. I'll be really honest with you and tell you I was not experienced at all in the sexual realm upon entering college. I think I had only kissed two boys by the time I arrived on campus. It was not for lack of interest or trying, that I can assure you. It was probably due to the fact that I spent seven years in an all-girls school, and any time I wasn't in school I was in dance class or rehearsing for a musical, and, let's face it, there weren't a whole lot of guys I was interested in, or if I was interested, they were definitely too old for me, or gay, or taken. I was also insanely picky. I consistently found flaws with any guy I was remotely attracted to or with any guy who was even the slightest bit interested in me.

Once I got to college, I made it a priority—right after getting cast in a show and getting good grades of course—to make it past first base. I am a quick study and had become decidedly less picky, so getting to second was not a problem, but that's where it stopped. I couldn't find anyone who I wanted to really be with me. I mean someone who wanted to be my boyfriend and fall in love and have a magical story about unicorns and rainbows where we made love for the first time. I was turned down by every guy I found interesting, even my best male friend. While I may have really wanted to have a boyfriend, I wasn't one to give up my principles for a guy. I didn't like drinking, especially not underage, and pot was also not my thing. Giving myself up to a random guy in a frat just did not interest me.

It turns out guys don't really want you when you are a twenty-year-old virgin. The idea that you might become attached afterward scares the living daylights out of them and they run for the hills. I learned that one night when I found a guy who I thought would be perfect. He was very attractive, was on the football team, and he had gay uncles. He seemed like a good guy, even if it was just for the night. The only problem was I made the mistake of telling him I was a virgin. After a lovely date at Panera Bread, where we were really hitting it off and having a great time, he brought me back to his dorm room and shuffled his roommate out, using some kind of bro-code that was not hard to decipher. Everything started off sexy and passionate. We were kissing and doing everything two people can do with all... well, most... of their clothes on, when I looked at him and said, "I have to be honest with you, I'm a virgin." You could have cut the silence with a knife. He stared at me for one millisecond and, in record time I might add, pulled me off his lap, pushed me out the door, and left me staring at the wall on the other side of said door, wondering what the hell had just happened.

I remember being embarrassed and ashamed, standing with my shoes, my bra, and my sweater in my hands. I hadn't realized the word "virgin" was a four-letter word to a college boy. I went to a small school, so I knew what happened was bound to make it around the football team like wildfire, but luckily, I didn't hang out with most of those people anyway. I was usually across the street in the theater department, where it was likely no one would hear the story of my complete and utter humiliation. I now realize that it was this guy who should have felt horrible for kicking me out in the way he did. If he didn't want to sleep with me, that was one thing, but throwing me out like that was another. No human being deserves to feel so completely rejected while half naked.

I told Dad about what happened, and he felt awful, too. He told me how stupid and immature that guy was and that he should never treat anyone that way. He told me I deserved a gentleman and that this dimwit certainly was not him. I tried to justify what had happened for weeks, but there seemed no explanation except for the fact that my virginity, at the ripe old age of twenty, scared boys away. After that semester, I stayed on campus to perform as Val in *A Chorus Line*. I dyed my hair platinum blonde as the part required and put on my biggest pushup bra in order to sing "Dance: Ten; Looks: Three," a song more lovingly known as "Tits and Ass." Gee, were my parents proud. They really were, although they joked about how I was consistently cast as either the bitch or the whore (true story). As my parents did every summer when I performed in my school's summer stock, they came to live in a house on campus where the college let them stay for the six weeks I would be in rehearsal and performances. They came to every single show, all fifteen performances, every summer. They are dedicated like no other parents I have ever met, without acting like crazy stage parents. My friends loved having them around and they threw the best cast parties, so no one ever seemed to think it strange that my parents followed me across the country every summer when everyone else was running away from their families. When your family looks different already, acting different doesn't really catch people by surprise as much, it seems.

One night after rehearsal, my dads and I went to dinner, just the three of us. Theater kids can get pretty crazy, especially when everyone in the cast lives in the same dorm for six weeks and spends virtually every minute together—it becomes like *Big Brother* on steroids. I needed a break, and luckily my parents were there to share it with me.

I was, once again, venting to them about how I could not find a boyfriend and Dad, much to Daddy's horror, said, "Honey, I think you just need to get laid." Daddy and I stared at him in shock. I knew

Dad was abrupt about sexual matters, but I was pretty sure that wasn't something most parents—at least, most good ones—advised their kids.

He followed that up with "I think I made sex too big of a deal for you while you were growing up. I was just so scared of you getting hurt or contracting some disease or getting pregnant. I didn't want anything bad to happen to you. But I think I scared you. You're so responsible. I know you would always take care of yourself, and I don't want you to have a broken heart, but I think honestly, the best thing for you would be to get your first time over with because it won't be beautiful, and it just needs to happen."

As crazy as this advice was, coming from my loving father, I knew he was right. I had built it up so much in my head, and it was becoming too important to me that it be perfect. And let's face it, no one's first time is perfect and anyone who says theirs was is lying.

So, I chose my victim, one of the two straight guys also performing in *A Chorus Line*. Despite dealing most of the weed that existed on campus, he was a nice guy, and he was a friend of mine, and I trusted him to be just that: a nice guy and a friend. I did not want anything more from him, I sure as hell did not want to be in a relationship with him, and so I thought he would be the perfect person to figure all of this sex stuff out with. I was dealing with a lot this summer. These weeks were also the weeks leading up to my Daddy's sentencing and a lot was going on in my head. Somehow, I thought having sex would make things less complicated.

Well, as it turns out, the only thing sex does not do is make anything less complicated. Let's call my victim Ronnie. Having learned my lesson, I did not tell Ronnie that I was a virgin, so it came as a surprise to both of us that there was so much blood involved. Since he was a friend and had several sisters, I decided blaming it on my period would be the best way to go about keeping up my pretense. Since he was my friend, he decided not to embarrass me by admitting he knew it was a lie. He was a quiet guy, but when we were intimate, he was caring and sexy, which I really had not expected, given that he also performed juggling in the on-campus circus.

I will spare you the long and rather boring details, however, Ronnie ended up also sleeping with a friend of mine while he was still sleeping with me, almost daily, that summer. It was an unfortunate affair. Regardless, I would not change the way I lost my virginity, or who I lost it to, even with the whole mess that followed after the night it actually happened. I discovered that I decide what I get to do with my body and it is *only* my decision. Some people may say I threw my first time away or that I didn't have enough self-worth or that I didn't prize my body for what it's worth. I disagree. I chose exactly how and when and what I wanted to do. I defined what sex meant to me. It was my choice and no one else's.

© © ©

My friend, the decision to have sex, no matter how many times you've had it, is not one to take lightly. No one other than yourself gets to decide with whom, how often, or how you should have sex. I feel that because I hold my body's worth in such high regard, I did not lose my virginity. I delicately placed it aside when it was no longer of use to me. I defined and continue to define my worth. You also get to define your worth and the worth you feel surrounding your body. Whether you're struggling with your body image or the ideals, or in some cases, laws, society has placed on your body, ultimately the way you feel about yourself is up to you. It can take years of therapy, soul searching, and unpacking, friend, but you have an opportunity to define your body's worth. Family, friends, society, or religion may have tried to tell you what you can and cannot do with your body, but that doesn't mean they get to. You define your worth, my friend. Your body. Your decisions. Your beliefs. You are worthy just as you are.

© © ©

What are some choices you can make for your mindset around your body today and every day that make you feel worthy?

CHAPTER 20

SURPRISING ANGELS

"Love is the only prayer I know."

—**Marion Zimmer Bradley,** *The Mists of Avalon*

I t was sweaty and hot in the dance studio theater at Muhlenberg College where I was rehearsing for the summer production of *A Chorus Line.*

Finally, our director called out, "Okay, take a ten!"

Phew, I thought. I was waiting for an insanely important phone call from Dad. It was supposed to be a great call—a call that would change everything. It would put behind us almost a decade of investigations and an indictment, and we could take a breath and get on with our lives. Finally, Daddy and Dad would be rid of this nightmare. After what seemed like an eternity, Daddy would officially be free.

The minutes ticked by, and still, my phone wasn't ringing. Why did this process have to take so long? I was going nuts. There was champagne and cake waiting for me at the dorms, for a post-rehearsal celebration of Daddy's sentencing, for which my parents had traveled to Hawaii. Maybe some probation, likely a hefty fine, but apart from not lying for them, he had cooperated with the government in all other aspects and the prosecutor had even recommended he get a minimum sentence. How could anything bad happen?

The stage manager called us back in, and just as I was about to drop my iPhone into my bright yellow dance bag, it started to vibrate. I looked down at the caller ID to see Dad's picture, and I knew that this moment was *the* moment. I could not wait. I had a close relationship with both the choreographer and the director, and they knew I was expecting the call. I told the stage manager I had to take it, and I would be back in one minute at the most.

When I picked up the phone with a cheery hello, Dad's voice was shaking.

"Hi, Chels. I'm so sorry, Baby. I'm so sorry. It's not good news. Can you sit down?"

My heart immediately fell into my stomach. I told him I was sitting. It was a lie, but I just wanted to know what was going on. The absolute worst-case scenario that our lawyers had predicted was that Daddy might possibly get three months' jail time. I reminded myself that was as bad as it could be, which would be awful, but I'd been prepared for this outcome. Three months with Daddy in prison and then all would be well again. Life altering? Yes, but we could handle that. It would suck, but it was not the end of the world.

"What happened?" I asked slowly, unconsciously delaying the inevitable.

There was a long-drawn-out pause before Dad answered, "It's so much worse. It's two years."

I cried out. It was the kind of sound that comes from deep within that you have no control over, a reaction to something you never saw coming. It was the sound of my heart breaking for the first time.

"This isn't right! They're wrong. This is wrong. This isn't how the justice system works. They're supposed to be fair. This isn't fair. How is this fair?"

"I know, I know, Baby. This is not fair. We will get through this together; we are stronger than they think." My Dad uttered this through tears he was trying to hold back.

How could my sweet, darling Daddy be subjected to this, my hero? The man who took care of us and provided for us, the most caring man I'd ever met, he could not possibly be going to prison. He had made a mistake, absolutely, but he had never, ever profited from this mistake and he was abundantly repentant. I had watched him beat himself up daily over what he had done and how it had affected our family. I feared this sentence would push him over the edge.

I said, "I have to go, Dad. I'll call you later. I'll be fine, I promise. My break is over. Tell Daddy I love him." Without giving him a chance to respond, I ended the call so he wouldn't hear me sobbing.

Until this moment, I had never understood what the physical manifestation of heartbreak felt like. The kind of pain that could be inflicted from something that wasn't physical at all. I fell to my knees and cried and cried and cried. They must have been able to hear me from inside the rehearsal studio because my friend Henry came running out, found me in the lobby, picked me up off the floor, and hugged me tightly. When a girlfriend of mine walked out of the studio, he seamlessly handed me to Gianna. She held me while I wept. She told me it was all going to be okay and whether I believed her or not, I do not remember. But somehow, in these deepest darkest moments, the Universe sometimes sends angels. My angel at this moment was a janitor for the performing arts department, a woman I had never seen before. She saw me barely able to take a breath in and walked over to where Gianna and I were standing.

She had the most sincere, understanding eyes I'd ever seen, and she asked, "Did someone die?"

I told her through muffled sobs, "Nnnnno, mmmy dddaddy has to go to ppprison."

She knowingly nodded her head and responded, "Ohhh, domestic violence?"

The idea of Daddy causing any kind of violence was so crazy to me, I actually stared at her and started laughing.

"No," I said. "Tax fraud."

She got me out of the horror of that moment and had me thinking about how much worse it could be. She was my angel in the weirdest of ways.

Like a true performer, my "show must go on" attitude kicked in, and I walked back into the studio to finish the last hour of rehearsal. Tears filled my eyes as I attempted to sing, and I did my best to blink them away while Henry squeezed my hand. I managed to sing my part and willed myself to get through the most painful hour of rehearsal of my life. After the rehearsal ended, I walked up to Charlie and Karen, the director and choreographer, whom I had worked with many times, and who knew my parents very well. My puffy, red eyes gave me away as I told them I was sorry for the interruption, but that my Daddy was going to prison.

Charlie responded in true Charlie fashion, "Which one?" My head was swimming and for some reason, without thinking, I answered, "The little brown one." My Daddy is on the shorter side, with a dark olive complexion, and tans incessantly, and apparently in my sad stupor that's the description that came to mind because sadness is not that concerned with political correctness.

"Oh, Chelsea, I am so very sorry," said Karen empathetically. "Do you want to come stay with me? I'm not sure you need the drama back at the dorms."

"Thank you so much. That is amazing, but I think I would rather just be with my friends and try to sleep and pretend this isn't happening, but I'm so, so grateful."

The news traveled quickly around campus, and several other faculty and staff members, as well as some friends' parents, even offered to come and pick me up, even though they lived more than three states away. I was so touched by all of these gestures, but I couldn't fathom not being in a place I knew when my whole world was feeling shaky.

It is in these moments that you realize who is there to support you and hold you up when you need help. I called my best friend Juliette and she immediately got in her car to make the drive down from Jersey to be with me. Meanwhile, my friend Angela would not leave my side. Whether I was going to the bathroom or sobbing in my bed, she was right there with me. My friend Julia checked on me constantly, making sure I wasn't drowning in my own tears. When I got back to the dorm after rehearsal, I saw the cake and champagne sitting on my desk—a bitter reminder of what was supposed to be—along with the receipt that my roommate asked me to reimburse her for. I picked up the cake and popped the bottle of lukewarm champagne alone in my room. I never drank much, and for a minute I thought about how ridiculous I must look with the bottle of champagne between my feet and the cake sitting on my lap. I laughed out loud. I laughed because I did not know what else to do. I felt grateful for my amazingly wonderful friends and my incredible family that I knew would not be taken down by this terrible news. I laughed because if I didn't laugh I would have cried. Angela climbed into bed with me and rubbed my back until I fell asleep. Juliette was there the next morning and kept tabs on me any time I was not in rehearsal. She knew all I wanted was hugs and love and for her to let me cry, to let me wallow, and then to try to make me laugh. She did all of that and more. I felt blissfully blessed that on this dark day I had so many beautiful angels to help me see the light.

One month later, after I finished performing in *A Chorus Line*, I flew back to Los Angeles and to my dads. I celebrated my twenty-first birthday on July second, one of my favorite days of the year. However, as things so often do in life, they got worse before they got better. Then, just one week after my birthday on July tenth, my alarm went off at four o'clock in the morning as I lay in my bed back in my childhood bedroom. The sound of the alarm made my stomach do that weird drop again. Dad knocked on my door to make sure I was awake. We did not really know what to say to each other so "I just wanted to make sure you're awake" was appropriate, I guess. I rolled out of bed and got in the shower, letting the hot water pour over me. I did not want this day to happen. I didn't want it to be over, either. I just wanted to go back: to hit rewind or reverse or something that would make it all go away. I got out of the shower and tried to focus on what I was doing in that moment and nothing else. Just dry yourself off. Just pull your jeans on. Just put on your Converse and go down-stairs. Just wait in the car until Dad and Daddy are ready. The time seemed to go by so slowly, and it also seemed to fly.

We drove up Interstate 5 for what seemed like an eternity, but after about two hours, we arrived in the middle of the desert in front of a gray building surrounded by barbed wire. We did everything we could to distract ourselves. We played happy music, we talked, we giggled about the time that would come after, when Daddy would be home with us again. We avoided thinking about spending the next two years of our lives separated involuntarily.

As we pulled into the prison driveway, the song that came on the radio was "There's No Place I'd Rather Be" by Jess Glynne. It felt so utterly ironic and we all laughed, and then the importance of this moment really hit us, and there was silence. We sat in the car and asked each other, "Okay, are we ready?" What a stupid question. Of course we were not ready. How do you get ready for something like this? We walked inside and Daddy checked in at the front desk. They said someone would be out to bring him in shortly. How ridiculous was that? You literally had to check yourself into prison. It was like the worst kind of summer camp ever, and I had been to a really terrible summer camp where I had to take care of goats that did not like me.

While we sat there, waiting for my Daddy to be taken away, a prison guard was checking in an older Asian man. The soon-to-be inmate did not speak English very well, and the way that prison officer treated him made me nauseous. It was as if he wasn't human. He wanted to bring in his heart medication, but inside of the medication container was one of those tablets that keeps the pills fresh, and the guard was yelling at this poor guy that he had to take out the tablet. The guy did not understand. The prison officer was screaming at him, and the man's wife was almost in tears. As if taking your freedom is not enough, they have to snatch your dignity, too. When I looked over, thinking about chiming in to help the man, the guard looked at me in a way that made me think I would never speak again. I started to cry. I so badly did not want Daddy to see me cry because I knew how hard it would make leaving us for him, but I couldn't help myself. It all felt so horrific. I felt sick. I could not leave my Daddy here with the possibility that people might treat him this way. He may have made a grave mistake, but he was still a human, and it wasn't like he'd been charged with murder.

When it was Daddy's turn, he brought forward the only two things he was allowed. Cash for commissary goods and his wedding band. When the guard asked him what he was going to do with all that cash, Daddy being Daddy said, "Buy deodorant." I could tell that the guard didn't want to crack a smile, but he did.

Daddy was so strong in spite of what was about to happen to him; he kept on a brave face. He was even making jokes. I clung to the hope that it would not be as bad for my daddy in there as it was for the other guy they had checked in. I prayed that maybe he would get by and possibly even make a friend who would take care of him. After all, these were not dangerous criminals. Most of the inmates were in for white-collar crime, or they had spent so many years in the criminal justice system that they had worked their way down to a minimum-security facility and were on their way out. I had to believe it was all going to be okay because if I thought otherwise, I was not going to be able to walk out of that building without him. I was not going to be able to actually face the fact that my Daddy was in prison.

The mind is smart, though, and helps you cope. It helps you cope so well that it's almost more painful to think about it now, looking back, than it was going through it then because the mind knows how to numb the pain when it is necessary. It knows how to block out what is staring you in the face and force you to turn your head and look elsewhere, for better or for worse, even if just for the time being.

That was that. We hugged Daddy one last time. We knew we would be able to see him on visiting days, but we didn't know what that would look like or when that would be, nor did we know that before he would even make it to the facility he was supposed to be in, he would be stuck in solitary confinement for a month due to a Bureau of Prisons "clerical error." (They make a lot of those "mistakes" by the way.) It is better not to know these things before they happen. As they say (anyone know who "they" is?), ignorance is bliss. I will never forget the moment they walked Daddy away. Tears were running silently down my cheeks, and he turned just before he disappeared down the cold, blank corridor and gave us the sweetest, bravest smile. His beautiful brown eyes said, *Don't worry about me, I'll be okay.* My heart broke yet again.

Dad and I drove home shell-shocked. I am not sure we talked at all, which is really weird if you know my dad and me. We got back to the house and lay down together in my parents' bed. We did nothing but sleep for several hours, but when we realized sleeping was not going to change anything, we decided maybe an episode of *So You Think You Can Dance* would distract us just enough to get through the night. Of course, the second we turned it on, they were dancing to one of Daddy's favorite songs. Dad started weeping uncontrollably. It was unbearable. This could not be what the next two years would look like. So, I turned to him, without really even knowing what I was saying, and said, "He didn't die!" Dad stared at me. At first I thought I had made a huge mistake, and then he began to laugh. He laughed so hard he was crying again and then I was laughing, too, that what-is-our-life kind of laugh. The most painful and necessary kind of laughter there is.

That summer, after returning home from losing my virginity and performing *A Chorus Line,* was the slowest-moving summer of my life. In August I headed back to Pennsylvania to complete my senior year of college. It was like I was living an oxymoron: a part of me gleefully celebrating my senior year with my friends while the other part of me was always waiting anxiously, holding my phone, waiting for the Caller ID to flash "Unknown" across my screen, knowing when I picked up it would tell me there was a call from an inmate at a federal prison and I would have my fifteen minutes to talk to Daddy.

We lived in this in-between space for two years. The space where if we were not laughing, we were crying, and sometimes the crying and the laughing bled together. It was especially rough for Dad when I was away at school. Though it was unbearable and suffocating at times, we also managed to enjoy ourselves because that is who we are: people who take deep breaths and always believe the future will be brighter. Dad visited Daddy every single weekend, making the eight-hour round-trip drive no matter what. Daddy received the only furlough in the history of the prison, which allowed him to attend my college graduation. We had our own miracles that year amidst the intolerable. My Dad was committed to my Daddy in a way that no one had ever seen at that prison, or perhaps anywhere. They were unbreakable, we were unbreakable, and we knew we could come out stronger on the other side. We chose to define our circumstances differently than they might seem to others. We chose to find joy regardless of being apart. We had learned how to do those things from Daddy.

⊚ ⊚ ⊚

I thought the whole time Daddy was away our lives were going to look like a pit of depression, but if I learned anything from these circumstances, it is that humans are so incredibly resilient, and also that even if someone you love is going through the hardest thing in their lives, it doesn't mean that you shouldn't also find joy and celebration at times, too. For a little while right after Daddy went away I was convinced that I just had to be depressed. That if I was happy, somehow he didn't mean as much to me, but I realized pretty quickly how much more Daddy would've suffered if he thought we stopped having fun or experiencing joy just because of what we as a family and he were going through. Friend, you can open up space for all of your feelings. Whatever you are feeling in any given moment is valid.

All emotions are valid and no one has to validate them for you. The fact that you're having them is your experience and whatever experience that is, is valid regardless of what someone might tell you. You are not too sensitive, too much, too anything. It might be that other people are uncomfortable with your emotions, but that is on them and not you. You are a freaking Rock Star for allowing yourself to feel your emotions even though we've been taught that emotions are not for feeling, but for stuffing. You are part of what is going to create change for generations to come. By revealing your emotions to others you are subliminally telling the world that, regardless of your gender identity, feeling is a common human experience and we are all in this together. It may take time for society to catch up to you. But I'll be here with you, feeling right alongside you, every step of the day.

© © ©

What are some ways you can start validating your own emotions instead of looking to the outside world? How might that change the way you allow yourself to feel?

CHAPTER 21

NEVER SERVE THANKSGIVING DINNER ALL ON ONE PLATE

"Happiness can be found even in the darkest of times
if one only remembers to turn on the light."

—Albus Dumbledore/JK Rowling

When it came time for the last Thanksgiving break I would have before graduating college, Dad and I hemmed and hawed about what to do. Daddy was away at his adult mandatory sleepaway camp, as we jokingly named federal prison. We had spent every Thanksgiving since I was eight in Mexico, and as of late Dad had spent every weekend in a prison visiting room and I'd spent any time I wasn't at school in Pennsylvania in that same visiting room on the weekends. I was tired of this prison ordeal, and yes, I know that sounds incredibly selfish of me. Daddy was sleeping in an airplane hangar filled with one hundred and twenty bunkbeds occupied by men who had done everything from submitting a false loan application to running the largest methamphetamine operation ever busted in the state of California. Here I was, whiny little me, just wanting to enjoy my senior year of college. I wanted some form of normalcy for Thanksgiving, but nothing was going to be normal without Daddy there. The amount of time I had off from classes did not really justify flying all the way back to the West Coast, so Dad and I settled on a quick weekend trip to Miami. We arranged for Auntie and my grandparents to visit Daddy so he would not be lonely, and the two of us jaunted off for a much-needed respite.

I met Dad at the airport in Miami and we checked in to the hotel, where we found that Daddy had, via Auntie, ordered champagne and chocolate-covered strawberries for us. Even though we had left him to fend for himself on a holiday weekend, there he was still putting us first, letting us know he was happy we'd gone on the trip together even though he couldn't be with us this year. However, from the minute we landed, something was off. Dad and I are not only very, very close, but we're also ridiculously similar, which oftentimes leads to us butting heads. Typically Daddy is there to break up the argument. He swoops in, making us both feel heard and validated, and before you know it, Dad and I have made up and all is well again. But without Daddy as a buffer, all hell can break loose on occasion.

Dad and I were missing Daddy big-time. We plastered smiles on our faces and tried to enjoy our time on the beach, but it just felt wrong, and we weren't talking about anything going on in our minds. A part of our hearts was broken. We are also pigheaded, and thus not so good at admitting our heartbreak. We just kept on muddling through with fake happiness, which was a big mistake. *Never* fake your happiness.

It all came to a head at Thanksgiving dinner. Dad had booked a lovely meal at a beautiful restaurant. Now, I am a traditionalist who likes things to always be the same, which is ironic considering that my whole life is nontraditional. Given that our favorite person was in a federal prison camp and we were thousands of miles away in Miami, there was nothing about this holiday that could feel the least bit traditional. The food came and it did not taste like what I was used to. I missed the stuffing we always had and the turkey the way I like it. It was all bunched there on one plate, and, even worse, it was fancy. Thanksgiving, in my book, is not supposed to be fancy. Well, I don't remember how it got started, but Dad and I got into a massive fight. I am *pretty* positive I started the argument. I was behaving like an ungrateful twenty-something who wanted her life back, when that was a clearly self-absorbed move and also not an option. Dad was putting on a good show while his heart was breaking inside. The person he had shared every moment with from the time he was twenty-five was no longer readily accessible. Nor were his hugs or kisses or reassurance that everything was going to be okay. We were broken without any glue to fix us back up. Dad and I got into it and it was not pretty. I was screaming in the middle of a nice restaurant, and Dad was so horrified and embarrassed that I was screaming, he stopped speaking altogether and we ate our dinner in silent anger.

All I wanted was to call Daddy. I knew he would have the words to make me feel better. However, you cannot just call an inmate in the federal prison system. They have to call you. So, I sent Daddy an email that I knew would take at least an hour and a half to reach him because every single email is first read by a prison official, and then

I had to hope Daddy was checking his email. I knew the chances were pretty good, given that it was three hours earlier in California and there's not a whole lot else to do when you are incarcerated. Sure enough, about two hours later, I got a call from Daddy. I was sobbing, absolutely inconsolable. I complained to a man in prison. Can you believe that? I went on and on about how awful I felt Dad was acting, which was totally unfair of me, but that's how I felt in the moment. I was hiding in the bathroom of the hotel room I was sharing with Dad, and I could hear him crying on the other side of the door as I relayed to Daddy what I believed his transgressions to be. Suddenly I heard the two beeps signaling the call was going to end. It was much too soon. There was so much more to say. There was so much more comfort I needed. "Chels, I will call back as soon as I'm allowed, okay?"

Without fail, thirty minutes later, he did call. I continued my litany of bitching, and finally he said to me, "Baby, I know. This is awful. All I want is to be with you and Dad. I am so sorry I did this to you."

That stopped me in my tracks. Daddy thought he did this to us? I couldn't bear the thought. I knew that between calls he was crying himself, beating himself up for getting us into this mess, wanting more than anything to fix things and take all of our pain away. Wanting to trade anything to go back and change his actions. There I stood, a college senior, free to live my life as I pleased, unloading my issues on this man who had already buried himself under a pile of self-hate and grief. Again we were cut off and again he called back when he could, but this time he called to hear Dad's side of the story. There he was gluing us together from thousands of miles away while behind bars.

After Dad got off the phone, he walked in the bathroom. I collapsed in his arms and sobbed, "I'm really sorry Dada. I just miss Daddy so much."

"I know, Baby, I know, me too." Dad stroked my hair and rubbed my back through a stream of his own tears.

We knew we had gone at each other for no reason. We apologized to each other. We should never have held on so tight to our boxes of emotions in front of each other. We should have let them run wild and free before they had to force their way out themselves. We were not helping each other or Daddy by trying to process things on our own. We are stronger in teams. We are stronger when we become vulnerable, especially around those we trust.

☺ ☺ ☺

My friend, when you're going through a major emotional challenge, or really a challenge of any kind, it is so easy to displace your emotions onto the people you love. When you feel so angry and you don't know where that anger should go, you can sometimes hurl your anger, rage, frustration, disappointment, and sadness at those who are closest to you. When we try to be strong by hiding our emotions we can inadvertently hurt people. That's why it is so much better to let your emotions run through you and allow yourself to feel them as they come up because they are going to force their way out of you one way or another, and if you're not dealing with them, you're much more likely to have them surprise you and not in a cute way. If you are not used to processing emotions or allowing yourself to feel freely, I would highly suggest a journal. Take time to freewrite without judgment of what you are writing. Set a timer for however long you want—I usually do about five to ten minutes—and just let your words flow out onto the page. If you're more of a verbal processor, find someone you can vent to and set some parameters. Let the person you are venting to know that you do not need to be fixed nor have your problems solved, but that you want to feel heard. When they know that, they are less likely to try to fix your problems for you when you are just wanting to get out of your head for a little bit. Venting is not complaining or bitching and moaning but a great way to release some steam on the pressure cooker that is your mind. And as always, I recommend therapy. I have been in therapy for years. I am not broken and I do not need fixing, but I find that I can benefit from introspection and understanding why I am the way I am. There is no shame in therapy, but there are endless possibilities for growth. Emotional intelligence is sexy, friend. Trust me.

☺ ☺ ☺

What are some ways you can open yourself up to introspection in your life? How might that strengthen your relationship to yourself and others?

CHAPTER 22

THE MAGICAL STORY OF A PRISON VISITING ROOM

"The world is full of magic things,
patiently waiting for our
senses to grow sharper."

—W. B. Yeats

D ad and I got in the car and made our way up I-5 to visit Daddy at "camp." It was something Dad did every single weekend. It was something I did when I had the courage. We knew we'd be in the car for four hours so we decided to listen to some audio books, this time Mindy Kaling's *Is Everyone Hanging Out Without Me?* was the breath of fresh air we needed. It was a different drive than it had been a year and a half before. We had been here. We had done this. We knew the road like the backs of our hands. It would be hot in Merced, it always was, no matter what time of year. We made our traditional stop at In-N-Out. We figured if we had to spend the

next two days in a prison visiting room, eating chicken pot pies out
of vending machines, we better stock up with some double-double
animal-style burgers, fries, and a strawberry milkshake for me.
It made us nauseous every time, like some kind of penance, or just
easier to think about our stomachs hurting than having to see Daddy
in a prison visiting room.

We pulled into the Courtyard Marriott Merced around dinner-
time. After eighty-some weekends Dad had spent there, he knew
everyone, and it had a strange homelike feel. We went to the local
"fancy" restaurant, the Branding Iron. It was our typical Friday night
haunt for some okay steaks and the best chef's salad there is. Then
we went back to the hotel to get Dad a glass of red wine and a molten cake for me. I treated myself to that cake every Friday night on
these weekends, as it seemed like I should get a free pass in terms of
calories if I was going to have to visit my Daddy in prison. We went
to bed early, watched an episode or two of *Friends*, and passed out
before ten o'clock.

Dad's alarm rang at 6:15 a.m. Time to get up and get moving. We
were never late to visit Daddy. We only had so many hours together,
and he looked forward to it every weekend, regardless of the fact that
he had to be strip-searched almost every time after visiting with us.
There was no way we were going to show up late. Dad and I moved
around each other comfortably in the small hotel room. We were
used to it at this point. Dad was always ready first and told me he
would meet me downstairs, so he could get a couple of coffees in
before we left. I met him about ten minutes later, desperate for my
latte. As a post-grad, I was not so used to getting up at six o'clock
in the morning anymore. Everything related to prison seemed to
always have something to do with an alarm clock. There was nothing

leisurely about it, since I guess leisure is not exactly what the Bureau of Prisons is going for anyway.

We left the hotel at seven-thirty sharp. Dad always made sure of that, even though the prison was only fifteen or so minutes away and they wouldn't let us in until eight. We sipped our coffees and joked and laughed. It was not weird anymore. It was just routine. Dad pulled the car off the freeway at the exit marked "Atwater." We drove through the fields and suburban homes that dotted the landscape until we saw the familiar towers and barbed wire. My stomach always tied itself in a knot at this point. Being on the prison grounds never got more comfortable. No matter how often I did it, it always made me anxious. The guards always made me feel like I had done something wrong, too. I knew my stomach would be like that for the next six hours, so I just gave in to the uncomfortable feeling. We pulled into the parking lot, across the street from the maximum-security penitentiary. Just in case you aren't familiar with the prison system, it's typical that on the same property as most maximum security prisons there is a minimum security prison, or "camp" so that when the maximum security prison goes on lockdown the "campers," aka inmates like my daddy, can perform the jobs the inmates on lockdown typically do. Their "camp" was a few Quonset hut-type buildings with a fenced-in yard, a mangy grassy field, and a basketball court. It was totally depressing. A few of Daddy's prison friends had lined up at the gate to wave to us. We could not talk to them, but we knew who they all were. Some of them had not had a visitor in over a decade, so for them, we were the closest they were ever going to get. I smiled warmly, trying to show them we cared even though there really was not anything we could do for them. We chatted with the other visitors in the driveway, usually the same people every time. They were kind of like our prison family.

We made plans to meet another inmate's family for dinner after the visit. Even though they barely spoke English, they always welcomed us like we were kin.

Then the door opened. They all let us go first since they knew if I was there, I would be desperate to see my Daddy. We handed over our IDs to the guard checking people in. We wrote down Daddy's inmate number next to our names, and then we were told to go in and have a seat, they would bring the prisoners in shortly. They told us which plastic chairs and small table to sit at.

I could not help but think that this day was far better than when we had to visit Daddy while he was in solitary confinement at the beginning of this whole process, due to the Bureau of Prison's error, which had instructed Daddy to self-surrender at the prison where a co-defendant from the same case was also incarcerated. Apparently having two inmates from the same case at the same prison facility is not allowed, but somehow the Bureau missed this little detail in my Daddy's case. However, since the system is for-profit, they kept him in solitary for as long as is legal before transporting him to a minimum-security camp where he belonged because the for-profit prisons make more money when inmates are in solitary confinement (your fun fact for the day). When we visited him in those days, he showed up in an orange jumpsuit, had lost a ton of weight in a matter of weeks, and was shackled at the ankles and wrists. We were forced to sit in a room that was all glass while other inmates, who were not in solitary, and their families would stare at us uncomfortably. Sometimes we were put in a different space where we were separated by bulletproof glass, unable to even hug. Compared to that, this experience felt like Disneyland. We had come a long way.

We gazed around at the large linoleum-covered room, littered with overused chairs and tables, and the five vending machines full of overpriced junk food that would serve as our sustenance for the next six hours. About fifteen minutes later, in walks Daddy. Always freshly shaven, his green prison uniform perfectly pressed and a massive smile on his face. Every time I saw his face when he walked in, my heart leapt. I forgot where we were. I forgot what we were doing. I just was so beyond happy to see Daddy in the flesh. He hugged and kissed both of us, just once—any more than that and we would have gotten in trouble. He would sit down next to me and immediately go into a litany of all the things he had done that week. What classes he had taken and taught. How many pull-ups he had done. The jobs he'd had, the interesting foods he'd learned to cook in the microwave, the friends he had made. There was always so much to tell when we visited. After all, we only got to speak to him on the phone fifteen minutes at a time, a few times a week, and in our family that is basically nothing. I think telling us all of these things was his way of saying, "Really, guys, I'm okay, I promise." Maybe it was a façade. We knew he was physically okay; we all also knew that he was tortured about the entire situation, especially in regard to how it affected Dad and me. Regardless, in the face of anything, Daddy can find the bright side. No. Matter. What. It's astonishing. Even in prison, he found a way to make his life seem not so bad.

I had been saving my surprise for Daddy since we sat down. I did not know how to tell him even though I knew he would be excited.

Dad and Daddy own a real estate company in addition to the accounting firm and business management companies. I had been auditioning all summer for various small parts in TV shows and student films, but I wasn't getting anywhere really, and I wanted to be able to move out and support myself. I wanted a job where I could continue doing my auditioning part-time, so I thought asking my parents for a job would be the best thing to do. It would only be a few months until Daddy came home and then I would get to work with him, too, which sounded pretty fun. Finally, Daddy stopped talking for a whole five seconds.

"I have something to tell you!" I slipped in. "I was thinking about getting my real estate license. I thought maybe I could work as an assistant and have a salary for a while, while I figure out this whole acting thing. Let's face it, to pay the bills I could sell lattes or I could sell houses!"

I think Daddy just about blew through the corrugated metal roof with excitement.

"Oh my gosh! Of course! This is perfect! I'll be home soon! We're going to have so much fun together!"

Then he started making plans for us and what it would look like when we would get to work together every day. Where we would go out for lunch. The clients he would want me to work with. He went on and on for the rest of the hours we had together that day and for the six hours we had the following day.

"That is a really good idea, Baby," Dad told me on Sunday as we drove back to Los Angeles. "I'm really proud of you for wanting to support yourself, but you know we are happy to support you while you find your way, too."

"I know, Dad, I just don't want to take advantage and the whole acting thing isn't really going anywhere and I'm kind of going nuts. I think I need to have somewhere to be in the meantime."

I had no idea what I had just gotten myself into.

My Daddy turned prison into a positive experience. Yes, you read that correctly. Since then, he has been my example of how to shift my perspective. Not only can he make lemonade out of lemons, which if you think about it isn't all that impressive, he can pretty much make lemons out of lemonade. While he was there he found ways to cope by continuing to grow as a person. He did a lot of work on himself. He started meditating daily, he worked out like a fiend, he learned Italian, he taught accounting and English as a second language to other inmates. He would run from building to building with other inmates yelling after him, "Duban! Where are you going?"

And he would respond, "I have so much to do today!" to which most of them would roll their eyes because *didn't he realize he was in prison?* So, whenever my perspective on things gets bleak, like the state of the world or our country, or I'm just having a rough day, I think about him. I picture him making the best out of a pretty crappy situation. He had a choice, as we all do: He could sleep away his sentence, or he could find some way to cope and maybe even enjoy himself a little.

ⓒ ⓒ ⓒ

We have a choice every single day. We get to choose how we experience every situation we are in. There are endless perspectives we can have when it comes to any one situation; why not choose a perspective that feels good? Why put yourself in a position to feel crappy? That's not fun at all. We have 100 percent control over our mindset. Every time we think we don't have enough of something it all starts and ends in our minds. It doesn't mean that you need to be Sally Sunshine when you aren't feeling like it, but if you notice you've been sitting in a low energy force field for a while, why not try a new perspective on for a hot second? It can't hurt to try. I know, you're thinking, but how, Chelsea? Well, here is one way I tend to pull myself out of those funks, after I've allowed myself to feel funky for a while. I brainstorm words or phrases about how I want to feel, for example, joyful, worthy, excited, or peaceful. Then I turn those words into "I am . . ." statements. Such as, I am joyful, I am worthy, I am excited, I am peaceful. I take these new mantras and put them all over the damn place. On stickie notes on my mirrors, my computer, my phone, anywhere you might see them as a little reminder. And when that isn't quite working, I go back to everything I am grateful for and everything I do have now. I also go out and have some good old-fashioned fun. Plan a game night, or call a friend, or pick up your favorite book. There are endless possibilities when you recognize that you are not at your best with situations, emotions, people, places, and things. You have power. So, take that power and go do something that makes you feel worthy with it because you already are worthy, you just have to convince yourself of it.

☺ ☺ ☺

What are the words you want to feel? How many can you brainstorm and turn into "I am . . ." statements for yourself?

CHAPTER 23

ᴛHE OᴛHER SIDE

"And the tree was happy . . ."

—**Shel Silverstein,** *The Giving Tree*

W e were back in the car on our way up to Merced once again, but this time it was different. Dad was flying up the freeway and our dog, Cambridge, was on my lap. Cami and I looked out the window as the orange groves flew by. The smell of manure was always particularly prevalent during this part of the drive.

"In a hurry to get somewhere?" I asked Dad, laughing as I spoke.

"Haha, very funny," he said.

I knew he was insanely excited. So was I. We had been waiting for this weekend for fifteen months. The plan was to put Cami in his pet carrier and sneak him into the Courtyard Marriott Merced, despite the no-pet policy. We would pull in the front and check in, and then when the coast was clear, I would bring the little puppy up the back staircase. Daddy had specifically requested Cambridge come with us to pick him up from mandatory adult sleepaway camp. Of course, he was the only family member that had not been allowed to visit. Daddy was finally done serving time and life was going to be what we had always dreamed it would be again.

Xay, the manager of the hotel, was there as we entered. "I can't believe this is it! We're going to miss you guys."

She handed Dad a basket full of snacks, which was so insanely sweet. She knew why we had been visiting so often and she and Dad had become friendly.

"We'll miss you, too," answered Dad, "but I'm pretty excited to have my husband home."

Xay had arranged a little goodbye party for us. In came all of our favorite employees from the hotel to say farewell. We exchanged numbers with some of them and promised to keep in touch. I went to get the little pupper from the car, first driving around back while Dad got the keys to our room one last time. I took Cam in and got him some water, and we immediately opened the snacks from the hotel employees. We were always hungry after that four-hour drive, and Dad was not one to stop while on the road. He always wanted to "just get there." Dad and I could barely sit still; we were too excited. Over time we had gotten to know Merced pretty well and had found a lovely little walking trail, so we decided to dispel some of our energy by taking Cami on a walk along the path. Even though it was November, the weather was still gorgeous. We sat and ate dinner outside at a nearby restaurant that we had found after we'd become a little sick of eating at the Branding Iron every single Friday. When we returned to the hotel after dinner, Dad had one more glass of red wine, and I had one more molten cake.

We did not need an alarm to wake us up the next morning. We drove onto the prison grounds and instead of turning for the camp, we turned toward the frightening penitentiary, where they process all the people who are being released. We put Cambridge in his Sherpa bag and hid him in the back seat. Dad and I walked in the front entrance and up to the guard sitting next to the X-ray machine.

"We're here to pick up Dennis Duban," we said together, proudly.

"Go wait in your car. He'll come out. You can't wait here," the guard responded without looking up from the desk.

Dad and I had gotten used to following the prison guards' orders, though they always made us a little jumpy. Some of the guards were pleasant, but some were total assholes (pardon my language, but there is no other word), and this guy was particularly nasty. Anyway, off we went to the car. Neither of us could sit still. We tried looking at our phones; five minutes passed. We tried talking about anything; ten minutes passed.

"Do you think they'll tell him where we are?" I asked.

The guards were not known for doling out information. I was a little worried Daddy might be sitting in the entrance, thinking we weren't here yet.

"He'll find us, Baby, I'm sure of it," Dad said not so reassuringly.

The time was passing, and Daddy was not coming out. We were getting pretty anxious, but the guard had said we had to wait in the car, and who were we to go against this guard's seemingly arbitrary wishes? All of a sudden, we looked up and there he was. Daddy. Tan and wearing a gray sweatshirt and gray sweatpants, holding the bag he'd been given to store his personal belongings. We practically jumped out of the car we were so excited. Daddy was beside himself. None of us really knew what to do. We were hugging and kissing, and then Daddy said, "Please, get me out of here." We hopped in the car and drove away, leaving Atwater Disciplinary Facility in the dust.

We had made it to the other side. The side we had only been able to dream of. The time after. Nothing could bring us down. A half-mile outside the prison entrance, I asked Dad if I could let Cami out of his bag. Daddy was so nervous that the dog would not remember him. He was four years old now and had only been two when Daddy went away. I unzipped Cam's bag, and he flew out and straight into Daddy's lap. He jumped up and down, one paw on either side of his face, kissing Daddy like crazy. Yep, I would say he remembered him. At some point, it was too much, and I put Cami to the back seat again and tried to calm him down, but he didn't want me, only Daddy.

Yes, it was the time after. We would be able to see him all the time now, but there were some more hurdles before everything would truly go back to normal. We were allowed eight hours to pick Daddy up and drop him off at the halfway house where he would have to live until they would release him on home confinement. While he did have his prison sentence reduced for good behavior, that did not mean he just got to go home. He had to serve the rest of the two years in a halfway house, followed by home confinement, until the full sentence had been served. Then he'd be on three years of probation. However, this was a step in the right direction. He would be allowed to work after the initial period at the halfway house. He could have a phone and call us whenever he wanted to. He could come home on some weekends. For sure, it would be better than having him behind bars and four hours away.

After about an hour we stopped at a Starbucks so Daddy could change. He had been so excited to get out to us, he hadn't even put on the civilian clothes he had to change into. When we walked into the Starbucks, immediately he started to panic. There were too many choices of things to order. He could not decide.

"Just get me something, Chelsea, please. I'm going to change."

I could tell he was overwhelmed. I guess I did not expect prison to change my Daddy, but it seemed that it had. Even with only fifteen months served, his perspective had shifted. Everything made him nervous; the whole world felt a little bit scary. He changed clothes and made his way back to the safety of the car. I handed him his asiago cheese bagel, and we were back on the road again. Since my apartment was closest to the halfway house, we decided to stop there to get Daddy some dinner before checking him in on the other end. He had asked that his sister and his parents be there to meet him. His only other request was for a steak. We pulled up into my building's parking lot and went up to my unit.

"Wow, Honey, it looks gorgeous!" he told me.

He, of course, had not been able to see where I had moved while he was away. His eyes filled with tears. He was so excited to be back, but so much had changed. It was way too much to handle all at once. Then the rest of the family showed up. Auntie, my little cousin, and my grandma and grandpa were there, and none of us could stop crying. We all just kept holding on to each other. Even though the worst was over, our ground felt shaky. The understanding that all of this could be taken away in an instant hung in the air. The only thing we had to hold on to was one another. Dad made Daddy his steak, and I am pretty sure Daddy's eyes were sparkling. He had not seen meat like that in over a year. We all watched Daddy eat an actual meal with actual fresh ingredients. The joy was palpable. The shaky earth started to feel more solid, and then it came time to drive Daddy to the halfway house. It felt like every time we were just about to adjust to a new normal something changed. *It could not be* that *bad,* we thought. We drove him there and in he went.

He called us from his cell phone the next morning. It was worse than prison, he said. It was disgustingly dirty. His roommates did drugs and were throwing up all night. They stole his wallet. He spent three months in the unkempt, somewhat frightening halfway house before he was finally allowed to return home to house arrest for another two months. Each step brought us closer to the end and offered its own set of challenges. While on home confinement, since he wasn't issued an ankle bracelet, he was called consistently during the day and night to make sure he was at work when he was supposed to be or home in bed when he was supposed to be. And at some point, no matter how much you love your home, it starts to feel suffocating to be that close to freedom but unable to truly experience it. Once he completed his time on home confinement, there would still be eighteen months of probation, half of which he would have to serve, again getting time off for good behavior. Then there were 600 hours of community service that he was to serve, which he did by tutoring students in business classes at a local city college—this was definitely the most rewarding part of the prison experience. The process seemed never-ending, but we could at least see the light at the end of the tunnel. More importantly, we still had each other. We had made it through prison. We could make it through this next chapter and certainly anything else that life might choose to throw our way. None of us would have anticipated that it would take almost five years for Daddy to feel like he was himself again.

It is really only now, as I am writing this book, that I see my Daddy as the man I always knew. Confident, funny beyond measure, and unafraid of the world. He also has a new caution when it comes to business, which I think isn't necessarily a bad thing. He has learned his lesson, that is for sure, and we have learned that we are unbreakable, and even when the ground feels more like quicksand than solid earth, we have each other to hold on to.

⟲ ⟲ ⟲

My friend, we will all find times when the ground feels shaky below us. We will all have moments when it feels like the life we've worked so hard to build is crumbling around us. In these moments, look around for what is still solid ground, and, no matter what, there is always something—a friend, a pet, a place. Go to places that bring you joy. Sit and breathe. Allow yourself to feel. Oftentimes allowing ourselves to feel those less pleasurable emotions can also lead us back to solid ground. But do not suffer in silence, find something solid to hold on to, or call a mental health professional. There is no shame in asking for help. What's most important in this life is that we are able to fully be ourselves as often as possible, and if therapy can help, why not give it a try? You will find your bit of solid ground amongst the quicksand. If you are willing to look for solid ground, something will appear.

⟲ ⟲ ⟲

What is your solid ground? Make a list of what you can grab for when you're feeling like you're in a good place, so that when things get shaky your list is already there and ready for you.

CHAPTER 24

WELL, HELLO THERE, MR. UNICORN!

"There are magnificent beings on this earth, son,
that are walking around posing as humans."

—Fannie Flagg,
Fried Green Tomatoes at the Whistle Stop Cafe

I pulled up and parked next to a massive hedge. Apprehensively, I got out of my car, careful not to swipe my clean nude-colored dress against my filthy car. I looked straight ahead and saw the FOR SALE sign and immediately had butterflies in my stomach. I told myself just to breathe, I was acting ridiculous, how hard could merely being a helping hand at an open house be?

The thing was, I had no experience whatsoever. Having graduated college with a degree in theater and dance, I never imagined myself here. I was hired, by my parents and their partners, as a marketing assistant, with no marketing experience, to the three Engel & Völkers offices they owned in Los Angeles, Santa Monica, and Beverly Hills and was studying for my real estate license. Almost shaking, I walked toward the gate of the house on Seventh Street in Santa Monica, listed at a mere, $11 million. Eleven. Million. Dollars. Who has that much money to spend on a house? I walked up to the gate wondering, *Do I ring the bell? Do I just go in? What's the protocol?* Ring the bell, I decided. Certainly, there was nothing wrong with that.

Sandra, the broker and my parents' business partner in the Santa Monica office of Engel & Völkers, opened the gate and welcomed me with open arms. I was a little surprised— this somewhat tough cookie was not often a hugger, but I wasn't going to second-guess any kind of kindness. We had met several times when I was home on breaks from college but hadn't spent a whole lot of time together before. She showed me around the house, how to open all the windows, turn all the lights on, things most people do not need to be shown, but in a smart house like this one, turning lights on was more complicated than anything I'd ever seen before. It was nothing short of programming that someone working for the FBI must have invented. If I left a door unlocked, she said, it would lose her the listing and I would be, as my grandpa would say, "in deep bandini." And I wasn't supposed to speak to anyone; if someone asked me a question, I was to refer them to her. I paid pretty close attention to these rules, but there was something distracting me. While Sandra was showing me around the house, a boy had quietly entered. Dominic was the new intern at our Santa Monica office, fresh off the plane from Nuremberg, Germany. I noticed he was handsome right away, but I was on a strict focusing-on-me-and-my-career mission and no guy was going to get in the way of that. He also looked like he was about seventeen years old, so I figured it was best to steer clear.

I walked up the cold, modern stairs to the second floor, where I thought I could find some peace and quiet to finish my very important job of switching lights from the off position to the on position. I was extremely anxious and even that seemed like a struggle. Then it was time to turn on the stereo for some background music. However, this dang stereo just did not seem to want to play. I went down into the basement to see if I could help Dominic because he did not seem to have the magic touch with the larger-than-life sound system.

Sandy screamed from above (not in a mean way, just in a you're-very-faraway way), "No! It's still not on! Oh, there it is! Oh, wait, it's gone again!"

Dominic's poor hands were shaking and I was beginning to think he was even more nervous than I was. Finally, thank God, Sandy decided to forgo the music. I headed back upstairs to man my post since we needed someone on every floor. I ended up surveying the upstairs most of the day, looking out the master bedroom window down the palm tree–lined street to the ocean—not half bad for a day job, I thought. Walking down the hallway, I was careful to avoid open house newcomers, God forbid I should speak to them. I was just security. I peered over the pristine glass barrier between the second floor and the first, careful not to put any of my smudgy little fingers with their damaging oils on the glass. Below me, I could watch Dominic standing as still as a statue, paralyzed by fear, welcoming visitors and potential buyers into the dramatic foyer with as few words as possible. He was kind but terrified, asking them in his adorable accent to please sign in. Finally, the torture was over: Dominic and I were released from our positions and we walked out of the house together, quietly parting ways, not sure when we would see each other again, but it did not really matter at the time; we hadn't even said two words to each other.

I was in an official "no boys right now" part of my post-grad life. I had dated a tiny bit in college after losing my virginity. Well, "dated" may be a strong term for what I was doing. I was hooking up, sometimes having sex, sometimes just kissing people. Never anyone totally random. All people I knew and mostly trusted, but it was discouraging. Just being physical with people wasn't enough for me. I wanted a real emotional connection, and every time I got close to really developing a relationship with someone it would fall apart. I had been told many times that I was the "marrying type" and that is "just not what I'm looking for right now" and that they "just didn't want to hurt me." Some version of that seemed to leave the lips of each person I attempted to get serious with (and by get serious with, I mean sleep with consistently for more than a month). Even when I would assure them that I didn't want to get married then, either, they didn't seem to believe me, thinking they understood me better than I understood myself.

There was one guy I had seen for a while and we seemed to really be hitting it off. Then as I attempted to make things a little more serious, I noticed him avoiding introducing me to his friends, refusing to hold my hand in public, like he was embarrassed of me, and that was something I definitely wasn't going to stand for—so I ended that right there. I was frustrated. I wanted to be loved and snuggled and to feel desired. I wanted a boyfriend who was proud of having me by his side. So, when I graduated, instead of getting frustrated by dating, I just did away with it all together. Sure, I would text guys on dating apps here and there, but I never met any of them in person. I threw myself into a new life instead, just focusing on me. So, as Dominic hopped on a bike in his perfectly fitting gray suit, and I stepped up into my dirty SUV and drove away, my mind was somewhere far away from the prospect of anything interesting happening with the hot German intern.

I went back to studying for my real estate license, Dominic went to work in the Santa Monica office, and several months passed. In the meantime, I officially started as a part-time marketing assistant at my parents' real estate company, Engel & Völkers. I worked most days in the Beverly Hills office, one day a week in their Hancock Park office, and every Tuesday in the Santa Monica office. I attended the meetings on Tuesdays only to find that Dominic, or Domi, as everyone called him, was still just as quiet as he had been on that first day we met in August. I started teasing him amongst the other interns, "Does he even talk?" To which the other interns would giggle, not really sure how to respond to the owners' daughter making this kind of gibe at the only male intern in any of the offices.

Time passed and suddenly it was the holiday season. Every year, the Engel & Völkers Santa Monica office is part of the Montana Avenue "Holiday Walk." The shops on Montana Avenue stay open late and E&V has a special tradition of bringing carolers in, offering cookies and Glühwein (a hot German spiced wine that is just as delicious and hangover inducing as it sounds), and providing a Santa Claus to take pictures with. Since it's such a large event, I was asked to come and help alongside the office interns to serve the Glühwein. Turns out it is a lot more fun to drink than to serve, and I am pretty sure I sneakily drank as many glasses as I passed out to guests, who were arriving in droves. Domi stood next to me, and I realized something I hadn't before. Maybe it was the alcohol going to my head, but all I could think was, *Man, he is handsome.* All of a sudden I had gargantuan butterflies in my tummy, and my mouth went dry. I had not met anyone even remotely interesting since graduating college.

I had been focusing on me, figuring out my career. This was not the time for love to intervene. My palms began sweating the more and more we chatted. It turned out all you needed to get Domi to talk was a touch of Glühwein and some holiday cheer. I also tended to forget that I was the owners' daughter, which could make someone a touch nervous, knowing that saying the wrong thing could possibly cost you your job, or in Domi's case, get you deported.

That night, after we had cleaned up, the younger crew from the office decided to go out. I have never been much for going out. I do not like being around drunk people, and I do not enjoy loud places, but one of the other female interns was going to be the only girl and begged me to go. What was I to do? Get very drunk was the answer, I guess. We first went back to Domi's place so he could change out of his suit and we could "pregame." Domi's studio apartment over the garage of someone's massive north-of-Montana-Avenue home left much to be desired, but for an intern only in the country for six months, maybe it was perfect. He did have a separate bathroom, but for some reason decided to start getting undressed in the bedroom in front of all of us. He took off his shirt to reveal two tattoos. I had never been so shocked. This quiet, very young-looking boy from the office was a rebel! Well, and damn, those biceps... I suddenly fell from my perched position on the couch, and by fell, I mean a full-on legs-over-my-head fall. Luckily I could blame this horrifying incident on the amount of alcohol I'd had to drink, and shortly after we all left for the bar.

Once we got there, I started to get uncomfortable. Some of the guys we were with were being way too handsy for my liking. As if I did not already find Domi adorable enough, he kept looking after me. Making sure no one bothered me, holding my drink when I went to the restroom, and overall just behaving like the most gentlemanly guy

I had ever met. We ended up sitting on the back of one of the bar's many sofas chatting. Domi was actually talking much more than I was—like I said, just a touch of alcohol and this guy became a Chatty Charlie. He told me all about his life growing up in a small farm town in Bavaria, and his recent travels with a friend all over the coast of Australia for six months. He talked about getting his scuba diving license in Thailand. He told me about his childhood and family, about the mischief he and his brother used to get into and how he had lunch every day at his grandmother's apartment. I sat there listening to his stories completely enthralled. He was flat out the most interesting and lovely person I had ever met. The night slowly wound down, someone sent me home in an Uber, and once I got home, I lay in bed not able to sleep.

No, not just because the room wouldn't stop spinning. I could not stop thinking about this German dude. He was cute and funny and smart and kind. I had just never met anyone like him. I was pretty sure this super-hot German guy was way out of my league, but I spent all weekend thinking about him. Daydreaming about what our lives would be like together, how we would spend our days, how he would know me better than anyone else. He would give me the cuddles I had always dreamed of and the forehead kisses I had always wanted. If I'd been in high school, his name would have been scrolled on every page of my notebook. I did not tell anyone that I was dreaming about the intern from the Santa Monica office because how often do stories about an intern and a boss's daughter have a happy ending?

I went to work Monday morning barely able to focus. How could this guy I had one conversation with occupy so much of the space in my head and my heart? I was pretty sure he had no interest in me, but I just had to take a chance, subtly at least. I tried to think of a way to get in touch with him. I could have snuck his personnel file from Daddy's office and got all of the information I would have needed, but that seemed a touch creepy for my taste. So I settled on sending Domi a harmless email. Here's the thrilling conversation that ensued:

From: Chelsea Montgomery-Duban
Sent: Monday, December 07, 2015 1:38 PM
To: Dominic Wächter
Subject: Wrapping presents is hard . . .
We need your help wrapping presents over here at the LA office… we're doing a terrible job and apparently you're the master.

From: Dominic Wächter
Sent: Monday, December 07, 2015 3:13 PM
Sorry for the late response, I'm about to unwrap most of our boxes and fold them. :D
Let me know how I can help you.

From: Chelsea Montgomery-Duban
Sent: Monday, December 07, 2015 3:19 PM
I'm just teasing because I hate wrapping :) …Im going to take about 10 with me tomorrow so don't unwrap them all!!
Man you get all the fun jobs don't you . . .

From: Dominic Wächter
Sent: Mon, Dec 7, 2015 3:42 PM
Haha yeah we already put boxes for you aside, of course just the best ones haha.

From: Chelsea Montgomery-Duban

Sent: Monday, December 07, 2015 4:01 PM

> Thank goodness! I hope you personally picked them out... okay just cut my finger on the tape... I am not cut out for this!

From: Dominic Wächter

Sent: Mon, Dec 7, 2015 4:52 PM

> Of course, just picked the best! Oh maybe you do need my help so you don't get more injured! :D

From: Chelsea Montgomery-Duban

Sent: Monday, December 07, 2015 5:02 PM

> Ahhh thank you!!! I definitely do!!

From: Dominic Wächter

Sent: Mon, Dec 7, 2015 at 5:20 PM

> Haha yeah, I'm pretty sure you'll make it!

So, clearly, I am a master of flirtation. This boy just had me so paralyzed by his perfection that I could barely put a sentence together. He asked me about my cut finger the next day, and I looked at him as if he had three heads and asked, "What finger?"

Here is a bit of advice, folks. If you are going to make up lies in order to flirt with someone, at least remember the lies you told, especially when they are in *writing*! God, I was so dumb. I hid a hand behind my back and said, "Oh yeah, yep, all better." He laughed a knowing laugh and we went on with our day. We kept in touch the next day via email as well, and this time the conversation got a hair more interesting, and I got a touch bolder:

From: Dominic Wächter

Totally forgot to mail/tell you that I'd like to come on 17th to the holiday dinner as well.

From: Chelsea Montgomery-Duban

Ugh you're the worst ;). Thanks for letting me know. Are you coming to the BH office party on Friday?

From: Dominic Wächter

Haha am I? :P

I would love to come on Friday, but I have to figure out if I can leave the office... someone has to be there until 6pm.

From: Chelsea Montgomery-Duban

Yeah... totally...

Ahh bummer... I'm only going to be there until about 6 because I'm going to that Realtor dinner thing.

From: Dominic Wächter

Yeah someone has to stay... but I'm going out afterwards with Mike and my brother, if you have time and want to join us you're more than welcome!

From: Chelsea Montgomery-Duban

Here's my number so we don't have to do this via email. I'd love to, but I have to go to that realtor dinner after the event on Friday here and I don't know when it's going to end... but are you pub crawling with Mike on Saturday? Cause I should be free Saturday night.

He could have found my phone number in my email signature if he'd wanted to, but what the hell, I had to be brave, right? I thought I was being pretty obvious; it turns out he had no idea for several days that I was even attempting to flirt...whoops. We started texting and yes, I did end up going barhopping with him, his brother, and his friend Mike that next Saturday, but before that he asked if I happened to be busy on Thursday night. I told him I had dinner plans with family friends, but (not so subtly) that I was wide open afterward.

I sat through dinner with my parents' friends on Thursday, overwhelmed with anxiety. They had put out the world's most gorgeous cheese board and cheese is my favorite food. However, those damn butterflies in my stomach would just not call it quits, and so much to everyone's surprise, I passed on the cheese and popped out the door before they started on dinner. With my heart in my throat, I drove the agonizing twenty-seven minutes from Bel-Air to Santa Monica to pick Domi up. Outside his place, I texted him to come down since the apartment over the garage did not exactly have a doorbell or legal permits (the things you learn when you get your real estate license). Domi came down the stairs and got into my car with a blanket, which perplexed me, since he said we were going to Top of the World, which I assumed was a trendy bar.

Like many tourists, Domi began to give me directions in my hometown, knowing much better than I did where to go without navigation. (I have lived in LA for twenty-seven years and still use navigation every time I get into the car.) We headed up toward Pacific Palisades. Now if you haven't ever been to the Palisades, let me set the stage. It is a quiet, residential neighborhood set in the hills up above Malibu—other than gorgeous views, stunning mansions with a few cute restaurants, and exactly one strip mall at the bottom of a hill, there's not a whole lot going on. It wasn't exactly where I would have pictured this cool joint I thought we were headed to, but I was merely the driver, and I went where he told me to go. We wound around the many streets that take you to the top of the Palisades, in the middle of all of these houses where it seemed the occupants had already gone to bed, and I began to think, this will either be the best date of my life or this intern is about to kill me and needs a discreet place to toss the body.

At the top of the hill on Lachman Lane, Domi told me to pull over and park. It was a dead end and there was nothing but hills, with the occasional massive house. Having thought we were headed to a bar, I was dressed in my tightest red jeans, a black blouse, and some killer high heels. I felt as sexy as I have ever felt until Domi said, "Now we're just going to climb that hill right over there." I tried not to look surprised or caught off guard, but I think the shock was embarrassingly obvious on my face. I asked him to give me a quick moment, and I furiously began digging in my trunk, thinking I had a pair of flat shoes I could slip on and feign readiness for a 10:00 p.m. hike. Much to my chagrin, I had just cleaned my car, which I never do, and I was forced to admit I had misunderstood the plan and was therefore ill prepared. Domi asked if I wanted to go somewhere else, and attempting to be brave, I told him it would not be a problem, I could hike in my heels. (I'm pretty sure I've never sounded more like a girl from LA than in that moment.) We took off up the hill and luckily it was a short climb. Thank goodness I was guided along every step of the way by Domi, my knight in shining armor. When we got to the top of the hill, the view absolutely took my breath away. You could see for miles, from Malibu to downtown Los Angeles—it was one of the most spectacular views I had ever seen. A viewpoint I had never seen my hometown from.

There is something you should probably know about me, if I haven't mentioned it already. When I get nervous, I talk, and when I say I talk, I mean a steady stream of words leaves my mouth, so that there is no possible opportunity for an awkward silence. We sat on Top of the World (ah, yes, now the name makes sense, doesn't it?) and talked about everything. Correction: I talked about everything while Domi, still very nervous about his English, listened patiently. Our hands slowly crept toward each other to the point where they were just ever so slightly touching, and the middle school–style butterflies in the stomach emerged big-time. I started to shake—it was cold, but more than that, this boy made me beyond nervous because I could already tell I liked him so deeply and there was some kind of energy between us that had me feeling that this would be different than the other guys. He wrapped his jacket around me, on top of the other jacket I was wearing, and he sat there in the freezing cold (well, as freezing as it gets in LA in the winter on top of a hill) while I talked my head off.

At one point I blurted out, "You know my dads are gay, right?"

If he had a problem with their gayness, there was no sense in us even continuing to talk. I mean that is a nonstarter.

He smiled and said in his adorable German accent, "Yes, I do."

I thought I might as well just put it ALL out there. "Okay, good. And you also know that my Daddy went to prison, right?"

That one is always more shocking than their homosexuality. I sat there thinking, *Oy vey, what have I done? This is way too honest for date number one.* I think Domi was shocked that I was so blatant about it, but he remained calm and collected.

"Yes, Ray in the office told me."

I thought, *And you still came on this date?* I have a trailer load full of baggage. I'm grateful that Ray, although he didn't know we were

going on a date, had told Domi about my Daddy upon his return from
camp and before his first day back in the office. Thankfully Ray did
some of the heavy lifting by explaining the whole prison situation to
Domi before Domi ever even asked me out.

After my outburst, he kept listening intently, laughed at all the right
moments, brushed his hand against my knee, and before I knew it, we
were lying down looking up at the stars together, huddled next to each
other for warmth—well, warmth was at least a really good excuse.

My nervous talking had taken me to a point where I was telling
him about a ladybug-shaped tent that I had as a child. "I loved it so
much," I said, "and once I decided to go camping in it, but I guess it
wasn't camping strength, and then in the morning . . ." And that was
all I got to say.

He kissed me, and I am pretty sure it was to get me to stop talking,
though I also don't think he minded it. The nervous butterflies were
fluttering at next-level speed in my tummy. I was both incredibly
excited and desperately trying to keep my cool, which I think made
me look like a caged animal trying to escape. I just could not contain
myself. The hottest guy I had ever had the pleasure of talking with
had just kissed me. It was like slow motion in the movies where they
kiss for the first time, and birds chirp and music plays and the whole
world stands still. And in your head, you think, *Oh my god, I hope
I'm doing this right, I'm so out of practice, maybe there's a new way that
people are kissing these days?*

I was doubly nervous knowing from my coworkers that Domi
had a bit of a reputation for being rather successful in the world of
dating apps and procuring dates. I guess what else are you supposed
to do on a six-month internship? We eventually came up for air and
decided after the tension had broken with the kiss that we should

probably head out. It was indeed freezing, and I had absconded with all of the warm clothing and blanket Domi had provided, so we headed back to his place.

Now, I had made myself a promise. I was not going to spend the night. I wanted to appear mysterious and hard to get. I was so intent on keeping this promise to myself that I had not shaved anything in like three days. I'm a Russian Jew. If I don't shave for three days, my body basically looks like a woolly mammoth and any prospect of sexiness is lost. I thought this would help me make good on my promise to myself. Well, as we arrived at Domi's place, he asked if I wanted to come in. My palms started to sweat and I knew I was not ready to say goodbye.

I said, "Okay, but just for a few minutes. I have to work tomorrow." As soon as we made it up to his apartment, I knew my resolution was over. He kissed me, and I lost every bit of inhibition. It was a strange feeling: I was beyond nervous but also so comfortable. He made me feel like a queen. We lay there on his bed, staring into each other's eyes, and well, I don't have to elaborate, you can probably fill in the details.

I have one very specific memory of lying there, in the arms of this most handsome human, feeling that I had found my new happy place with the boy I barely knew but somehow already loved. We listened to Bill Withers' "Lovely Day," and Domi swore that when he sings "lovely day" over and over in the chorus, it actually sounds like "Dominic" (listen to it, as crazy as it sounds, he's right), and we laughed and laughed and just enjoyed each other's company. I rolled over and tapped his phone to see the time. Almost 2:00 a.m. Shit. What was even worse, there were three Tinder messages waiting for me to leave so they could have Domi's attention. Major shit. What was I thinking? Of course this guy was just here for his internship. He could not possibly be serious. Why did I get so ahead of myself? I was immediately heartbroken, feeling cheap and stupid for sleeping with him. I was just one girl out of many. I had to get out of there as soon as possible. I told him I had to get to work early and needed to get going. I dressed and planted a cursory kiss on his lips. We didn't make plans for a second date, which only assured me that my suspicions had been correct. I ran down the stairs and to my car willing myself to hold the tears stinging my eyes, until I was out of sight. I cried the whole drive home.

When I got back to my apartment, my phone beeped: "Did you get home safely?" Maybe I was wrong... I let my mind spiral for another hour or so while I attempted to sleep. I woke up the next day waiting for him to text or call me. I was sure he was going to, then I was sure he was not going to. My friend at work finally looked at me (she was the only person at work who knew we had gone on a date the night before) and said, "I'm taking your phone away."

She was right; I was obsessing. It felt like the day was never-ending, and I looked at the computer and lo and behold, it was only 11:00 a.m. I decided I would text him after my doctor's appointment at one. I mean, come on, I already did not play hard to get, what was the point of keeping up pretenses now? I certainly couldn't mess things up with one text message. I managed to keep my heart rate down at the doctor's office, and the minute my appointment was over I looked at my phone. Amazingly, I was not going to have to text him after all because there was a text from Domi asking if I wanted to "hang out" again tonight. In this day and age, no one is brave enough to go on an actual date, and let's be honest, I did not care about the terminology, I just wanted to see this guy.

So I did see him, and then again the next day, and the one after that, and the one after that. Now I wake up next to this boy every morning and he is the person I want to share my life with forever. In case you're wondering, after he asked me to be his girlfriend, he deleted his Tinder account, as did I. Turns out after our first date he never went on a date with anyone else. Ah, the things we see in hindsight. If I had the ability to remember that hindsight is 20/20, maybe I wouldn't have so much anxiety about everything. Maybe if that little girl who always wanted a boyfriend and never had one knew that she would be the first of her friends to get married—to the most incredible human—she wouldn't have worried so much.

© © ©

As much as I hate to admit this, the future will never be a sure thing. What I do know is, that every time I look back, I find the Universe/ God/or whatever higher power you do or don't believe in put me exactly where I needed to be. The more we can let go, I know it's hard, but still, the more we stop trying to figure out and worry about the future, the more we can enjoy where we are right now. We can certainly do everything we can to manifest what we want for our futures, but not at the expense of being in the present. And manifesting is not the same as worrying. Shit happens for better or for worse, but these things make you who you are. They make you stronger and help you grow.

Your life and your story seem to have a funny way—sometimes good, sometimes bad—of catching you by surprise. In the end, the lessons you learn are what you need in this lifetime and, if you believe like I do, for the many lifetimes to come. Here's to great, big, messy, crazy love and all the other nuttiness in between. Like my Daddy says, "You woke up today looking at the grass from the right side; it's all going to be okay."

◎ ◎ ◎

How would it feel to let go of the future now and then and just be here in the present?

CHAPTER 25

Ho Ho Ho

*"And above all, watch with glittering eyes
the whole world around you, because the greatest secrets
are always hidden in the most unlikely place.
Those who don't believe in magic will never find it."*

—Roald Dahl

My family is super close. My dads are two of my very best friends and heroes. Domi, Dad, and Daddy are pretty much everything to me and all of their names (or what I call them, anyway) start with D's, so that is a plus. Not many girls are so lucky to feel this close to both their parents and their husband, and I do feel particularly blessed. I've heard people say that my relationship with my dads borders on too close, obnoxiously close, but it is who we are, and we love our life that way. My therapist insists on boundaries, and we are working on it, I swear.

The minute Domi and I started dating they knew about him beyond his being the office intern. I told them everything, even things they maybe didn't want to know, and I think they knew I was in love maybe even before I did. They knew their baby girl was not the type to mess around. Dad was even a little afraid as I went through high school and college with no serious boyfriends that I would end up a alone with fifty dogs and cats. But I was just looking for the "right one," not just the "one for right now." I was way happier on my own than I would have been settling for a relationship that did not fulfill all of my needs. I have a lot of needs.

When Domi met both his bosses (aka my parents) for the first time at the office holiday party, he didn't know that I had already told them that we were dating. Auntie was there, too. No one else besides my family and one or two coworkers knew we were dating. We were pretty good at hiding it (or at least, we thought we were good at hiding it). We figured until we knew where things were going, it would be best to just keep it between us. Domi also thought my parents were in the dark, so, when Dad walked up to him and gave him a massive hug, he was a touch confused. He wondered if all the Engel & Völkers interns received such warm welcomes from their bosses. Still, he thought he had the night to observe my family without them any the wiser when in fact it was the other way around. On the way back to the car, when I told him that they knew we were dating, he looked at me in utter disbelief.

"They know? And you didn't tell me that they know?"

I told him I'd just assumed he knew they knew... why would I not have told my parents? That's when he began to realize just how close I am with my dads.

About two weeks later it was Christmas, and on December 23, or really in the early hours of December 24, Domi had officially asked me to be his girlfriend after a whole ten days of dating. I was on cloud one million and nine. I had always wanted a boyfriend, and finally the moment had arrived—not just with anyone, but with the perfect one. The one who gave me butterflies and made me feel at home all at the same time. I slept at my parents' house on Christmas Eve so I could celebrate Christmas morning with them. I shared the good news that I was officially going steady with the coolest kid on the playground, and they were both very excited. My parents had always been the types of dads where if I am happy, they are happy, and without a doubt I was beyond filled with joy. They knew my relationship with Domi was different from any other fling, or short-lived relationship (if you could even call it that) I'd had previously by the way I was acting, and from the little they knew about Dominic in the office and what I'd told them, they trusted him. He was exactly the kind of guy my parents had hoped I would go for. Smart, kind, funny, well put together, mature, and also a little goofy.

I woke up on Christmas day feeling like something was missing. My usual Christmas cheer was just a notch off. I realized I did not want to spend the holiday without Domi. I asked Dad if I could invite Domi to dinner, and his eyes sparkled with that thrill parents get from their kids finding love. "Of course," he said. Daddy would have to rearrange the whole table and figure out the seating, but he would get over that frustration and the table would still be perfect. Most kind girlfriends would slowly introduce their new boyfriends to their families over time, at various occasions. I, on the other hand, figured it was sink or swim, Baby. Daddy, still living at a halfway house in Hollywood, had to be picked up, so I figured I would go get him and then grab Domi on my way back to Malibu. If I think about it now, I cannot imagine how unsettling it would be to have your girlfriend pick up her father, who also happened to be your boss, from a freaking halfway house, and then come and get you. Fortunately, I did not think anything of it at the time.

Daddy was overjoyed to be out for the night and to get to stay with us at home, so he was in an excellent mood. While we were driving, my phone kept buzzing. I knew from the fanfare coming from my phone that it was Domi. I asked Daddy if he could look at it for me since I was driving, and I am a rule follower (really, friends, don't text and drive).

Daddy looked and said, "Oh my God, is he the cutest or what?" Domi had sent me three photos of three different outfits—possibilities for dinner that night. I told Daddy to pick one and still, to this day, Domi does not know (well, I guess until he reads this) that Daddy was the one to choose his outfit that night, not me.

We arrived at Domi's apartment to pick him up, and as he came out the door, Daddy hopped in the back seat so Domi could sit in the front with me. Domi was horrified. He couldn't believe his boss was getting in the back seat so he could sit in the front. He begged Daddy to please sit in the front, but Daddy insisted we get to sit next to each other. "That's just how it should be," he said. Plus, if he was sitting in the back seat, he could catch up on his emails, which, I'm guessing, may have been his ulterior motive.

We arrived in Malibu to a houseful of people. Everyone on Dad's side of the family who lived within a fifty-mile radius was there. I may have understated to Domi before he decided to come how many people would be there that night. I should also mention that Domi was sick. He had a fever and felt awful, but sweetly (probably disgustingly so), it did not stop him from coming, which made me adore him even more. He quietly charmed one entire side of the family like it was nothing. I only knew he was nervous because, when he got up from dinner, his entire shirt was soaked. To this day he tries to blame it on the fever, but I know better. He was super quiet then and still not so sure of his English, but he did not have to say much for everyone to fall in love with him. My cousin Shannon, whom I've always had something of a cousin code with, even though she is thirteen years my senior, was giving me all the signs that I should lock him down as quickly as humanly possible, and I have always trusted Shannon's judgment when it came to these things. She grew up babysitting me and dancing to the Spice Girls. She obviously knew what was up.

I really wanted to stay the night at my parents' house since it was Christmas and all, and I assured Domi he could stay with me, but Dad told me that I should stop torturing the poor boy and just go home with him. So I did. Merry Christmas to me. Driving to Domi's apartment that night, I realized I had a newfound respect for him, throwing himself to the wolves like that. He wasn't just the shy guy I had initially taken him for. He was engaging, hysterical, and *very* charming. I also realized he was the one. Anyone who would be willing, with a 101° fever, to come and meet their significant other's family, complete with gay dads and a felon, and who tried to find the perfect outfit, must really actually like me.

© © ©

My friend, I'm going to let you in on a little secret. When I was fifteen, I was first introduced to what manifestation is. We had some friends who, after having listened to me whine and complain that I was never the girl with a boyfriend, gave me a scroll and told me to write down everything I wanted in a partner and not to leave any small detail out. So, I took the scroll into a quiet room and lit a candle. It seemed nice and symbolic. I proceeded to write out everything, and I mean everything that I wanted in my perfect partner. Things from having someone who would give me forehead kisses when I needed them, to being European, to being the kind of guy who would want to support me in all that I do while also knowing that I could do it on my own. Yes, I swear I was fifteen when I wrote these things. After about an hour and writing approximately one hundred and fifty characteristics that I wanted in my partner, I rolled up the scroll and hid it in a drawer where no one would ever find it. Seven years later I met Domi. He is European, gives me those forehead kisses, and certainly knows I can accomplish anything on my own, but he also supports me in everything I do with such pride and admiration. He is everything on that list (minus him not having blue eyes, which I can live without) and more. Don't tell him, but I'm pretty sure I manifested him. If nothing else, I got really clear on what it is I wanted. I did this again with my career before I left real estate, (oh yeah, spoiler alert, I don't work in real estate anymore) and a year later, I am living out those dreams. Writing out what we want, allowing ourselves to dream big and then letting go of the timing is such a powerful tool in attracting to us more of what we want, and I am here for it. Maybe it sounds a little woo woo and yeah, which it probably is, but I'm watching my sweet Domi right now, falling more in love by the minute, and believing in this manifestation stuff hard-core. You absolutely can do this, too. Allow yourself to dream big, the bigger the better, write down everything you have dreamt up, and then let go of the timing because that part is not up to us so much.

⊙ ⊙ ⊙

What is something you've been too scared to admit you want for your life? What would it feel like to believe that dream is yours for the taking? Who's to say that it isn't?

CHAPTER 26

ᑡHEILIGE BIM BAM

"Mein Deutsch ist nicht perfekt."
(My German isn't perfect.)
—Me, all the damn time

I have always been nervous about speaking foreign languages. For some reason, whenever someone asks me to do it, my tummy tightens up and my brain seems to fall out of my head, so that any knowledge I did have of said language is no longer there, and neither is my English. I took French all through high school and did well in the class, but once when I was traveling around France with my parents, Dad asked me to ask someone where the nearest bathroom was. I, of course, knew how to say the words, but for some reason, my mouth wouldn't form them. I couldn't. I refused. And Dad would not take no for an answer. I got so upset I started to cry. I could not understand why, but it just made me panic to even think about trying.

Then in college, I took one year of Italian before studying for several months in Italy. When I got to Italy, all of my friends decided I would be the best spokesperson for the group since I had the best grasp of the language. Everywhere we went I was the person who ordered and asked questions out of necessity, since we were in a small town where not everyone spoke English. I did it because I had to.

It seemed that languages would follow me wherever I went in life until I learned to speak one other than English confidently and without reserve. Shockingly, the Universe is even more relentless than I am. It will make darn sure you learn the lesson or at least the language. It just won't give up.

So when I met Domi, an actual German, and he told me, "Either you can learn German or our children will speak behind your back," I was initially taken aback that a twenty-two-year-old guy I had only been dating for about a month was willing to talk about a potential and very serious-sounding future with me. It made my heart do back-flips. I immediately got my booty into German lessons. Certainly, no one, especially not my own offspring, was going to be talking behind my back! I went every week to class and did well, even though German is a really tough language to learn because there are so very many rules. I just kept trying.

Then ten months after we started dating, when it came time for our first trip to Germany together, I panicked. I was back to being struck dumb with fear every time I heard German, and Domi was stuck with the role of translator twenty-four hours a day. A few days after we arrived in Nuremberg, Domi and I went to dinner with some friends of his I had never met before, and of course I wanted to make a good impression. So the stakes were already high.

We were sitting down to dinner when the waitress came over and said, *"Möchten Sie etwas trinken?"*

I stared at Domi with a highly confused look and the waitress then said, "Would you like something to drink?" I continued to stare at Domi: my heart was pounding, my mouth was dry, and I did not know what to do.

Domi looked at me and said, "Baby, she's speaking English."

Everyone cracked up. I went perfectly crimson. I could not believe that I was in such a panic mode I didn't even hear that the waitress had repeated herself in English. The fear of sounding stupid had overwhelmed me so much that I'd tuned everyone out and was just waiting for Domi to come to my aid. I felt so helpless and I never wanted to feel that way again when we visited Domi's hometown.

I finally realized that this in itself was my holdup: my terror of sounding unintelligent. Then I realized how hard it must be for Domi. In the U.S., he spends every waking moment of every day speaking in his second language. The least I could do would be to really try to learn his language in order to communicate comfortably with him and his family when we're in their hometown, so he doesn't have to spend all of his time translating between us. If his fifty-year-old mother could start learning English in order to communicate with me, I could, at the very least, return the favor. Learning a language takes dedication and time. Speaking it takes a ton of courage. You have to have zero fear of what you might sound like and whether someone might laugh at you. Now I look around at the immigrants in the United States with even more respect for their ability to communicate in a foreign land, in a foreign language, because it is so tough.

Domi came to the U.S. knowing English but he'd never been tasked with speaking it around the clock. When we started dating, English was our only option. We don't fight often, but when we do it's usually related to some sort of language barrier between us. Well, that, or how we believe our future children should be raised . . . .

One day shortly after Domi and I started living together, about three months into our relationship, we were grocery shopping. Innocent enough, right? Well, sometimes even when you speak the same language, communicating can be hard—now add the pressure of just having moved in together and speaking two different native languages. We just wanted to buy some food for dinner. We may have also been a bit hungry, and neither one of us is good at operating with low blood sugar. Okay... so we were both hangry!

"The rotisserie chicken looks good and we don't have to do much work," I said.

"Okay and let's get some feta, tomato, and onions to bake it with," Domi said.

"Why would you bake it if the chicken is already cooked?"

"No, you bake the feta and tomatoes and onions."

"I understand that," I responded, "but why would you put the chicken back in the oven if it's already baked?"

To which he replied, "No, we're going to make it with the feta."

Having now heard a similar phrase several times, I started to get a little annoyed.

"Why the hell would you bake the feta and the onions and tomatoes with the already baked chicken?"

What I wasn't understanding was that Domi was saying we would bake the feta, tomatoes, and onions separately, as a side dish. (At that point I had never heard of baking feta, so you can understand my confusion.) Domi got so frustrated trying to explain what he meant that he started screaming in gibberish, like a child having a tantrum, and sat down on the floor of the Vons. I was so embarrassed that I took one look at him behaving like a child and ran away to hide in another aisle. When I realized how ridiculous we must have looked to our fellow shoppers, I started cracking up and walked back to where I had left Domi on the floor of the produce section. He was laughing, too.

I said, "Just buy what you want, we'll figure it out at home."

For a while, most times Domi felt he had upset me, he would try to pull the language barrier card, claiming he didn't "understand what he was saying." I let him get away with this excuse for a while because, let's face it, communicating in a second language twenty-four hours a day is exhausting. However, when he started university in LA to finish his bachelor's degree and was getting straight A's, I decided enough is enough. There is no such thing as a language barrier between us anymore. What I have come to realize is that two people from the same country also suffer from this "language barrier" syndrome because we all communicate differently. Sometimes it is valid to use the language as a reason—even when you're speaking the same language—for why the other person seems to be making no sense at all.

I have come a long way in my German skills as well. Three and a half years after we started dating, at our wedding in Germany, I stood up in front of all of our family and friends and said my vows and gave a toast to my new family in German. I was very proud. I had worked so hard, and I was so nervous, but out of necessity I finally overcame my fear of speaking another language and, more importantly, my fear of sounding stupid. If my angel, in the form of Domi, had not helped me along the way, I would still be that scared little girl in Paris crying about asking for a bathroom (and my Dad would still need to pee), but because I found someone who supported me and only giggled a little when I made silly mistakes, I had the confidence to stand there and proclaim my love for him in his language.

ⓒ ⓒ ⓒ

Communication is so vital to human existence. What I have always found is that when the need arises for people to communicate with each other, even if they do not speak the same language, they will find a way. However, there is an insane gratification that comes with learning a new language if you're willing to put in the time and energy. Whole words that do not exist in English exist in German. It's like a new world opens up when you have the capability to express yourself in not just one language, but two. More importantly, learning a second language taught me that I will forever be a student, and I will never be perfect. And that is perfectly alright with me because none of us are perfect, or if you look at it from a different perspective, all of us are perfect in our own way. No amount of knowledge makes you better or worse than someone else. But if we open ourselves up to new knowledge of any kind, so many opportunities will unfold before us. It doesn't have to be something big like learning a new language, it can be anything you want it to be, maybe learning how to cook your favorite dish, or learning more about a country you'd like to visit. Recognizing ourselves as lifelong students of life opens us up to a world of possibilities.

ⓒ ⓒ ⓒ

What's something you've been wanting to learn, but have been too afraid to start? What's holding you back from starting? How can you overcome whatever it is that holds you back and get started?

CHAPTER 27

FOREVER AND THEN SOME

"Just when you think it can't get any worse, it can.
And just when you think it can't
get any better, it can."

—**Nicholas Sparks,** *At First Sight*

My Auntie had the best laugh in the entire Universe. The kind of laugh that always told me when she was at my performances because I could hear it ring out even when the jokes were not that funny. It all made sense when I found out she was my biological mom. I was the spitting image of her minus the fact that I looked like a giant next to her. (I used to borrow her shoes when I was eight and she was in her forties, if that is any indication of my enormously large feet or her insanely tiny ones.)

I think I took after Auntie in the sense that I do everything with all that I have and with all that I am. Even if I do not love what I am doing necessarily, I want to do it fiercely and with all the passion I can muster. Auntie worked for Daddy most of her life, and she always supported him passionately and worked harder than anyone else at the office. For many people, she was not the easiest person to get along with, mostly due to her loyalties to certain people and her ability to hold on to grudges for a lifetime. She was hard to please. But if you were in, you were in, and lucky for me, I was in. I think I had the least complicated relationship with Auntie out of anyone in my family. We had a sort of silent understanding. The kind of understanding you get to have when someone is your biological mom but owes you no responsibility. She loved me without question and without strings, and I may have been the only person in her family who she was easy (well, easier) on—not her kids, not her husband, not Daddy, and certainly not her parents. We just had this kind of magical bond no one else quite understood.

I called Auntie every single day on the bus on the way home from high school. We would laugh about the ridiculousness of that institution and the people who came with it. She always would tell me how proud she was that I worked so hard and continued to show up every day, no matter how people made me feel at school. I knew she had my back. I think she felt growing up that she was alone, even though that was not the case. I think she felt misunderstood and separated from the life she wanted. Auntie, Daddy, and Uncle Robert grew up in Skokie, Illinois, and when Daddy was eighteen, Uncle Rob was sixteen, and Auntie was eight, my grandparents moved the family to California. I am pretty sure Auntie never forgave my grandparents for moving because it took her away from her best friend. She made her parents' life pretty difficult through high school, but she was their baby, so their capacity to put up with her was enormous.

When I started working at my parents' real estate firm, it meant that I got to work in the same building as Auntie, which I adored.

We got to spend so much time together: coffee in the morning, lunch break downstairs, sessions spent complaining about coworkers. It was just like I thought it would be working in a family-run company. In my childhood, I'd played with Auntie's adding machine at her office, and somehow I grew up and came back to spend my days working with her. I ran downstairs to ask questions just because I could, spent way more time than I should have sitting across from her desk, and she would avenge my honor when my direct boss wasn't behaving nicely. (No wonder people hate the boss's kids . . .) It was amazing.

Here is another thing about Auntie: She hated going to the doctor. She avoided it like the plague because she was embarrassed that she smoked. She tried to hide her smoking from me, and then once I found out, she continued to hide it from her kids although I'm almost positive they knew. Auntie had a pain in her side for a while, and finally, when she was sick of all of us telling her she had to go to the doctor to see what was wrong because it had been months, she went. The doctor said it could be several things, but just to make sure, she wanted to run some additional tests. In those additional tests, they found a tumor on Auntie's lungs. They did some more tests to see what exactly was going on.

I was hanging at my parents' house after work one day as I often did when I knew Domi was going to be busy. Dad and I were sitting in his bed watching TV—I don't remember what we were watching. Daddy came in and asked us to turn off the TV. He said that, unfortunately, the tumor they found on Auntie's lung was malignant.

I asked, "How bad is it?"

He said, "Well, it's stage four, but she's going to fight, honey, okay? She's going to fight and we will figure this out as a family."

I could not understand him; it was like he was speaking a language I didn't understand. I asked him to repeat what he'd said a few more times. I did not know what to say, so I just walked out of their room and into my childhood bedroom to call Domi. I told him the news and he said something similar about fighting this battle and being there for my family, but I cannot even remember the call anymore. I hung up the phone and looked in the mirror in the room I had grown up in. I looked just like her. It was so weird. I would always look like her. She was in me and so we would fight this fight together. She was unbeatable, unstoppable. She was the strongest person and certainly the most determined person I knew.

So, we did. We fought together. I took her to almost every chemo appointment. I held her hand, knowing exactly what she needed. As we sat and waited for hours, I ordered soggy waffle fries from the café down the street. I would tell her jokes, and we'd plan trips together to every corner of the world. For our first trip, as soon as she was feeling better, we planned to go to Jackson Hole, Wyoming, just because it was pretty and we decided we should. We were going to sit in a big fluffy bed together in a fancy hotel and drink wine directly out of a box because that is just how classy we are. We made lots of plans and looked at tons of wedding magazines, as Domi and I were in the depths of wedding planning.

One day I took Auntie for a bone scan. It was at UCLA, which is like one giant maze. Auntie had started having a little trouble walking because of the chemo drugs, but she was doing okay more or less. We walked into the room that held a massive contraption where Auntie would lay down for the hour or so it took to complete the scan. She asked me to sit in the room with her while the machine repeatedly searched her body because the apparatus was scary, and she said she would feel less frightened if I was there with her. As she was going through the machine, we could both see the scans appear on the screen above her.

"What do you think all of that is?" she asked.

"Nothing," I said. "I don't think it's anything. I'm sure it's going to be fine; let's just wait for the doctor."

I lied. What I saw terrified me. Even as someone who knows nothing about medicine, I knew what I saw on that screen was bad. We got Auntie dressed, and I shuffled her back to the car, but when we got there she could not lift her legs into the car. I had to pick her up and put her in the front seat. I held it together, making her laugh all the way home. When I got home, I sat on the sofa, comatose. Domi came home and we watched one of our favorite TV shows together, but about halfway through the episode, I started crying inconsolably. Domi wrapped me in his arms and rocked me back and forth as I cried, "She's dying, Baby. I am watching my Auntie die." He just held me and let the storm pass. He knew better than to say anything to make it better because nothing could. I went to sleep and could not get out of bed the next morning. I cried for several hours. I mourned my Auntie because I knew she would be gone soon and I was scared. Auntie was my protector, my defender, devoted to me in her own way, like no one else. I could not bear to lose her.

When the results of the bone scan came back, the doctor informed us that the cancer had in fact spread to her bones and she would have about three months left. All of us chose not to believe that was the case. We had weddings to plan and to attend, children to celebrate, life to live . . . so we did—we lived life as if nothing had changed. We all pretended. We pretended well. Auntie was diagnosed with cancer in January. In October, Domi and I bought a house exactly seven blocks away from hers. It was wonderful. I had never lived near people I was close to before. My ten-year-old cousin, Rebecca, who also happened to be my half sister, and I could bond more than we ever had before, and I could take care of Auntie when my uncle had to go on business trips. I would go over there and make sure Rebecca got to bed, though she was pretty easy and didn't need much help from me. While Auntie lay on a hospital bed in her bedroom, I would rub her feet. We'd watch *Law & Order* because that was her favorite and talk for hours until my uncle got home. I would help Auntie to the bathroom and pick her up off the toilet when she was done and get her back to bed. The chemo had started making her really sick, so about two months after the scary bone scan she decided to stop. She got stronger and looked healthier and better than I had ever seen in the last year.

Before Dad, Daddy, Domi, and I left for our annual trip to Punta Mita, Mexico, for Thanksgiving, we celebrated Rebecca's birthday at my parents' house. I sat on the deck next to Auntie and looked out at the ocean. I put my head on her shoulder, and we sat there for what could have been hours, just watching the girls play and feeling each other's presence. The day before we left for Mexico, I went to say bye to Auntie, since we would be gone for ten days. I gave her a hug as I was leaving. She asked for just one more, and she was crying.

I told her, "It's okay, Auntie, we'll be back in a week and a half."

And she said, "I know, I'm just going to miss you."

I told her I had to go, I was going to be late for something.

Walking down the hall, I turned around and waved to her, and she smiled at me and said, "I love you, Chelsea."

"I love you, too, Auntie!" I said, and something in the way she looked at me scared me. It was a look that did not say just goodbye for ten days. I looked at her until I started down the stairs and until

I could not see her face anymore. I shook the nagging thought from my head.

That was the last time I saw my Auntie. The day after we got back from Mexico, Domi and I were on our way to a house showing at a listing of ours. Dad called me as we were walking up the block, just a few minutes before the showing. I picked up, knowing I could tell Dad I would call him back later.

"Hi, Honey," he said.

"Hi, Dada! How are you? I'm running into a showing, can I call you back?"

"Baby, I'm sorry, but I have to tell you, are you with Domi?"

"Yes, I am." I swallowed hard.

"We just lost Auntie this morning, Baby. She and Uncle Willie were dropping off Rebecca at school and then as they were driving to the doctor for an appointment, we lost her."

I screamed and wrapped my arms around Domi's neck and held on so tight because I did not know what else to do.

"We lost Auntie," I told him. "She's gone."

I saw the look in his eyes, too. He was going to miss her like I did. He was going to take on my pain, too.

"Oh Baby, Baby, okay, I am so sorry. I will go cancel the showing."

"No," I said, "go do it, but I'm going to sit in the car."

He told me he would not let me, and I told him that it would be okay. I walked up to the house and told the agent we were meeting that I had just gotten the news that my aunt had passed away, and as humanity is, at its core, really kind, she hugged me. Someone I had never met before hugged me and her eyes told me she really meant the good wishes that were coming out of her mouth. She asked if we wanted to cancel and I told her that luckily we are a team and Domi could do the showing without me. She wished me well and Domi watched me walk all the way back to the car with worry in his eyes. I could tell he was positive he shouldn't leave me alone, but I promised him I would get on the phone with someone and that I would not just sit there. I called my soon-to-be brother-in-law, who was also living in Los Angeles, first. I told him I didn't really want to talk but that I'd promised Domi I would stay on the phone with someone, and he was okay with that, so we just sat in silence connected by a phone while I waited to figure out what life would look like without Auntie. I told him I should keep calling people to keep myself busy and he made me promise that if I couldn't get in touch with someone else I would call back.

I called my best friend Juliette and left a message, and my friend Rebecca and left a message, and then I called Dad back. He and Daddy had been put in charge of figuring out what to do since Auntie left no will or information about what she would want. My uncle could barely function, so my parents got to work. Finally, Domi was back. He asked me what I wanted, so we drove home and got in bed together and let *Friends* play all day in the background while I slept and cried on repeat. Dad called and told us that Uncle Willie and Rebecca wanted to have dinner that night. So we went to Rebecca's favorite restaurant. My beautiful eleven-year-old cousin was so strong, just like her mom, and she made me strong with her. I never saw her shed a tear. She was stoic and determined to keep moving. I made her giggle and we joked all night long about the awful peanut butter–banana burger I had ordered. I looked at Rebecca and made a silent promise to Auntie that I would take care of the family she left behind: Uncle Willie and my cousins, Alex and Rebecca, who are simultaneously my half siblings, and who I'm so insanely proud of.

Auntie got me through so many tough times in life, and she believed in me like no one else could. I was her miracle. I wanted to be that woman for Rebecca. Instead of falling into a dark pit of depression, I decided I wanted to be the woman my Auntie would want me to be: strong, independent, and a protector of others. So I let myself cry about missing her when I needed to, but mostly I tried to carry on her legacy of bringing the family together, of protecting those she loved, and of loving myself just as fiercely as she loved me because I know that is what she would have wanted. She left behind two incredible kids: Alex, who travels the world as the most dedicated chef I know, and Rebecca, who is still figuring out who she is in the world. Their lives should not stop just because their mother's did. They deserve to live beautiful lives.

My friend, we all have a path in life, and we cannot protect each other from those paths. We will each have our own struggles and our own wins. The way my younger cousins handled the death of their mother with such grace was an example to me that we can all carry on, even in life's deepest, darkest moments. Rebecca's friends rallied around her and she's now flourishing in middle school. She is an accomplished dancer and somehow puberty is treating her kindly. (I'm insanely jealous.) Alex is in Australia, living his dream of traveling and cooking. He stayed home for a few months after Auntie died, but then he got back to pursuing his dream, and I am so proud of him for that. We can all learn so much about continuing to live in the wake of losing someone you love from these two. My friend, life goes on no matter what, and we have the choice to keep facing it and find what is beautiful in the world, or to hide, and the choice is entirely our own. It is our choice to live, our choice to love, and our choice to learn—and it is also our choice to bury our heads in the sand. It was Auntie who taught me about laughing uncontrollably, living passionately, and loving fiercely. Auntie will live in me forever and ever and then some.

© © ©

Wrap your arms around those you love. Tell people how much you love them. What is holding you back from fully expressing your love for those who you're surrounded by?

CHAPTER 28

I LOVE YOU TO THE SUN AND THE MOON AND BACK

"And I think if you're going to be with somebody,
you owe it to them to show yourself."

—Chris Crutcher,
Staying Fat for Sarah Byrnes

M y alarm had not gone off yet, but I could not sleep. How could I? It was the day I had dreamed of my entire life. I was going to marry my very best friend in the entire world. I tossed and turned in the bed next to my maid of honor, Juliette, staring at her, willing her to wake up. She slept with earplugs and an eye mask on —obviously I did not have a chance. Since I never wake people up directly, my best hope was my alarm and that was still thirty minutes from going off. I had so many butterflies in my stomach I couldn't tell if I was going to start flying or throw up. I was not nervous about marrying Domi. I was beyond excited. I wanted to take in and remember every single moment. My parents had rented this gorgeous villa, large enough for a sizable family to live in, for my bridesmaids and me to stay in the night before the wedding, and I kept waiting for someone to wake up so I could run around like a crazy person and be excited with someone else.

I heard a door—someone was awake. I chased Alex down the hall, trying not to scream and wake everyone else up. She and I made coffee and talked about how insane it was that I was getting married. Then out came Olivia. We sat and chatted and hugged. All braless and giddy, just like in college. We watched the sun rise high in the sky and looked out at the ocean. It did not even feel real, but I tried to really take it in. Finally, Juliette woke up and the four of us just sat on the deck in awe. We couldn't wrap our heads around how we all of a sudden grew up. All these years together huddled in dorm rooms and now we were sitting on the deck to the most gorgeous suite and one of us was getting married. This image will be emblazoned in my mind for all time—all of us there, the quiet of the morning, the hum of anticipation. I felt their love and support. I felt their arms around me, and as the coffee started to kick in, I could no longer sit still. They're my girls and they know me. So they let me talk and talk and talk and then talk a little more and get all the nerves out. Even though two out of the three of them would rather die than wake up early in the morning, they all sat there bright-eyed and bushy-tailed and ready. They truly dedicated their hearts and souls to me for the entire day, and I'll be grateful to them for that always.

We got dressed while we blasted, as only theater nerds would, "An Old Fashioned Wedding" from *Annie Get Your Gun* and sang at the top of our lungs. Then we headed down to the bridal suite where breakfast and hair and makeup were awaiting us. I could not have imagined a more perfect day. You spend all day getting pampered, and then at the end, you are ushered down the aisle to the most wonderful man in the world. Just thinking about it now gives me butterflies all over again. It was funny: I expected to cry a lot that day, and I did not. I laughed a lot and danced around a ton in my underwear, but I wasn't crying. Right before the ceremony, when we were back in the bridal suite, everyone gathered except for the groom and the groomsmen to get ready to walk down the aisle. We had about fifteen minutes and Charley, our phenomenal wedding planner (yes, the same incredible woman who ten years prior had planned my parents' wedding) said, "It's time to put your veil on."

I was initially against wearing a veil at all, so it surprised me when the minute they put it on my head, I broke down in tears. I looked in the mirror and thought, *I am a bride.* I wasn't playing house, I wasn't dreaming, I was really getting married and starting the next chapter of my life. It was almost too much emotion to handle. I asked my girls if we could just go to the bathroom together and take a minute. We all stood in a circle, crying, and then I looked at them and said, "You're all still going to be my friends, right?" They cracked up—it was such a ridiculous typical Chelsea question—of course we would all still be friends. It's just that no matter whether it is the best change in your life or not, it's still change, and it's still scary, no matter how sure you are of the person you are going to meet at the end of the aisle. I will hold that moment—all together laughing and crying simultaneously—in my heart forever. They were not going anywhere. I had made sure of that, so now I was ready to go and marry my guy.

From my little corner in the bridal suite, I could see everyone lined up. All the bridesmaids and the groomsmen, my grandparents, Domi's parents, and best of all, Domi. There he was with his mom, arm in arm. Just the back of his head made me catch my breath. My heart was pounding. I thought it might leap out of my chest. I watched them all walk away from me and up the aisle. I looked out at the sea of guests who had come from all over the world—friends and family, old and new—all there to support us. Not a dry eye in the place. I felt filled with love.

"It's time," whispered Lottie, Charley's fantastic assistant, who was dedicated to me all day long.

I lifted my ridiculously heavy, gorgeous bouquet and pulled along my seventeen-pound dress and walked to the top of the aisle. My dads would be meeting me halfway down (you have no idea how long that aisle was). I heard the fanfare from the live trumpeters (yes, I truly live in a fairy tale) and knew that was my cue to go and stand at the top of the stairs. I took a moment. I took a breath. I looked at the ocean. I saw my dads and I knew I could do this. By this, I mean walking down the stairs alone without being able to see my feet and hopefully not falling on my face. I made it to my parents and gave them each a kiss. We linked arm in arm as we'd always done, and then all I could see was him, my unicorn, my future, my everything. There he was crying and looking at me the way I had always dreamed someone would look at me. I had missed him all day. I couldn't help myself—I had to say hi and wave my hand at him like some silly little five-year-old—but hey, it was our wedding, I could do whatever I wanted.

I locked eyes with Domi at the beginning of the ceremony and never looked away, except maybe once or twice to take a peek at the golf course that was our backdrop, and the ocean beyond the grass. I remember thinking, if this is my future, just this man and me, even if everyone and everything else melts away, I would have everything I want.

Walking back up the aisle, though, elated as I was, when I looked at the smiles on the guests' faces, it hit me that there was one face I would not be seeing. I missed Auntie that day. I had never imagined I would have a wedding that she would not attend. Shortly after the ceremony concluded, Auntie Melanie found me and asked if I saw the seagull that had hovered over the guests for the entirety of the proceedings. I had not although I knew who it was. She was right there watching from the best seat in the house. I knew there would be no way she would have missed this moment in my life. The same warm tingly feeling I felt the day I found out Auntie was my biological mom surged through my veins once again.

Now, you do not get a lot of time alone at a wedding, but we did our best with the time we had…no, not that…get your head out of the gutter! We went back to the bridal suite and shared a lovely moment where I gave Domi a music video I had made of me rapping along to a German rap song and he gave me a diamond necklace. We had another moment, just us, right before we entered the wedding reception, where I started to panic a little bit. I think I was overly exhausted and had been anxious all day, or maybe all year, and it caught up with me. I was having a hard time breathing, but my sweet husband put one hand on either side of my neck and placed his forehead against mine, and we closed our eyes and he whispered to me, "It's just us, Baby, no one else, it's just us."

I looked at him and smiled and gave him a big bear hug. He was right: This day was all for us. There was no one to impress, no certain way we had to act, we just had to enjoy being us, being husband and wife, holding hands, and feeling proud of our commitment to each other.

He told me without telling me, "There's no way to mess this up, Baby, because we did it, we have each other, and as long as we have that, we can get through anything."

Apparently, even our wedding reception.

Some people wonder why we (or really, I) wanted such a big wedding. It was not really about the party. I mean, the party was amazing, but it was about the chance to celebrate with the people we love and the chance to declare our love in front of those around us, a chance to stand up in front of everyone and say, "Hey, we're choosing each other, so if you could root for us and help us when times are good and when times are hard, that would be great." A wedding is a process that can bond you as a couple, if you can make it through the stress of it all, and help you understand how to work together and take care of each other. It's a time when you can take stock of who stands by your side, and who maybe falls away, even though you thought they would be there for you. And I would be lying if I did not say that, for me, it was also a bit about pleasing that little girl inside of me, with the two gay dads, who always wanted to be a princess.

☺ ☺ ☺

My dear friend, there is no one way to live your life. There are endless possibilities. Just because someone says that something is "supposed" to be a certain way does not mean that they know best for you. There would be so many things in life I wouldn't have done if I had listened to what I was supposed to do in each season of my life and there could have been even more things I would have done had I really let go of what other people think. What can I say? I am a work in progress as we all are. What I do know is you are so very valuable to this world. You are so special. There is not a single other person like you and the world is blessed to have you. You live your life the way you want to, not the way anyone else or society tells you. If no one has done things the way you are doing, then congratulations, you're blazing the freaking trail. If you follow the path of thousands before you, incredible, you are forging your own way in their footsteps and that's a beautiful thing, too. There is no one way. There is no right way. There is what is best for you and you are the only person who knows what that is. I love you and don't you ever forget that we define our own worth.

ⓖ ⓖ ⓖ

What would happen if you let go of everyone's expectations of you and allowed yourself to live the life of your dreams? Tell me, my friend, what then?

EPILOGUE

Here is the deal. Sometimes life is a fairy tale. Sometimes it very much is not. The one constant is that people are always going to have opinions about everything, especially about other people and what they should be doing and who they should be. People will always be giving other people labels and attempting to put everyone else in boxes. The other thing I know to be true is that other people's opinions are totally, 100 percent, out of your control. What is not out of your control is your reaction to those opinions and how they affect the way you choose to live your life. No one else's opinion of you, or your actions, or the labels they give you should ever dictate how you feel about yourself, nor whom you decide to love, nor any of your decisions. If my family and I had listened to other people and what they labeled us, we would not be a family. Daddy would not have made it through prison with the positivity he did, and none of us would have fallen in love, and I would not be writing this book. You are brave. You are important. So take the opinions of others under advisement—sometimes they are really helpful—but please, at the end of the day, know the only opinion of you that ultimately matters is yours, and the only label you ever have to go by is one that you choose.

I was created out of an impossibility if you think about it. At the time, the way my parents had me seemed like something that could never happen. Two gay guys having a baby that was related to both of them? I was made because my parents believed they would create a child, no matter what anyone in the outside world said, so it was easy for me to believe that anything is possible and that I could have anything in the world I wanted. Because I believed that, it became my reality. Even at times in my life when it didn't appear that I was getting what I wanted, when I really looked inside, I could see that I was attracting and creating exactly the life I wanted and needed. The Universe was taking care of me.

When I look back, I see a pattern. The times I was most successful in achieving my dreams were either times I completely, 100 percent, believed I could have something or I deserved something, or times when someone told me I could not have what I wanted.

When I was a little girl, my dream was always to be the Sugarplum Fairy in *The Nutcracker*. In high school, my dance teacher told me I was not strong enough to dance en pointe with a partner, but instead of breaking me, it motivated me. No one gets to tell me what I am or am not capable of. No one gets to label me weak nor decide my worthiness for me. So, not only did I wake up at four in the morning before school three times a week to train and make myself stronger, but having been told I couldn't do it only solidified my belief that the Sugarplum Fairy was mine to be had. There was not a shred of doubt in my mind... most of the time. Sure, if I had been a different person and my dance teacher told me this was an impossibility, maybe I would have believed it, but because I am a creation of impossibilities, there's no room in my mind to believe that I cannot have something. And lo and behold, after writing down on a small piece of paper that

I would be the Sugarplum Fairy, folding it up and tucking it away in the back of my desk drawer, and years of strengthening myself and dedicating myself to becoming the best I could be, I was cast as the Sugarplum Fairy in *The Nutcracker* my senior year of high school.

Anything is possible, my friends, not just for me, but for you, too. Throughout my experiences in life, the following principles have helped me find my purpose and achieve my dreams while maintaining inner peace.

1. I define what success looks like to me, knowing that it will not necessarily match anyone else's idea of success, and I allow this definition to change as I grow and change. To me, success is where my greatest joys meet my greatest strengths.
2. I believe my dream is mine for the taking.
3. I write down exactly what I want and see myself achieving that goal or getting that thing.
4. I let go of the timing of it because timing is the Universe's job, not mine.
5. I never lose faith. Every time I was dumped or I loved someone who did not love me back, I never said, "I'm never going to find love, I'm a lost cause." I always said, "Damn, that sucks, but okay, I can be sad about this for a little while and then I am off in search of my perfect person. If it's not this person, it's okay— my guy is out there and we will find each other. I just know it." And look who showed up. You define your worth, friends.
6. In the meantime, while I am waiting for my dreams to come true, I have fun. I dance in my car. I sing at the top of my lungs. I watch my favorite movies. I find joy in the silliest things.
7. I am grateful for everything I *do* have right *now*. I am grateful

for the tiniest things, like the perfect cup of tea, and I am grateful for the most massive things, like having found the perfect life partner.

8. And then, when I do get exactly what I want, because the abundance of the Universe will always provide, I am grateful for it every minute and every second of every day.

People don't call me Sally Sunshine for no reason. I am positive to a fault. I have full faith and I do not let setbacks get me down. Yeah, some crazy things have happened in my life, but I am living proof that anything is possible, and if I can have everything I want in life, so can you. Just try it, okay? Believe wholeheartedly in yourself and what you want, don't lose faith, be grateful, have fun, and never give up. You already have your greatest gift: you. So just decide you can have everything you've ever wanted and believe nothing is an impossibility. If you ever doubt it, just think about those two guys who took a leap of faith in 1992. Anything is possible. Anything can be yours. Now go and be *Inexplicably You.*

"There are only two ways to live your life.
One is as though nothing is a miracle.
The other is as though everything
is a miracle."

—Albert Einstein

ACKNOWLEDGMENTS

T hank you, friend, for reading this. Thank you for sticking with me on the journey I've had thus far in life and learning lessons alongside me. Remember, we don't have to go through life alone. Do not suffer in silence; that isn't strength, it's just suffering alone. Reach out. I hope together we can start to define who we are by our own standards and not anyone else's and find joy and gratitude along the way. I love you. I am hugging you. I am so grateful to you for taking the time to get to this page in my book of life. Thank you.

Dad, oh boy. I quite literally would not be who I am today without you. I admire you, appreciate you, and love you so very, very much. Thank you for reading every iteration of this book, remembering parts of my history I had forgotten, and pushing me to be the best version of myself every day. And thanks for being a disciplinarian—trust me, it was worth it and we all know Daddy wouldn't have done it. It is an honor to be your daughter and a hell of a lot of fun, too. I love you beyond measure.

Daddy, my sweet Daddy, it is because of your unconditional love that I have never settled for less than I deserved. It is because of you that I know what gratitude looks like and because of your example that I know what it means to follow your heart, and your passions, and see the glass half full. Thank you for being you and for loving me the way you do, and for hugging me so hard I may just pop. I love you forever and always.

Domi, my love, you quite simply make life everything I've ever wanted it to be. You support me, cherish me, and give me the forehead kisses I've always wanted. My unicorn, I couldn't ever imagine spending my days any other way than by your side. You bring me more joy than I even thought was possible. These words aren't enough, but I know you know what I mean. And please never lose your accent, it's super sexy. Oh, and thanks for the idea that I should write a book…good call. I love you to the sun and the moon and back and then some.

Auntie Melanie, thank you for being the first person to ever read the first version of this book. Thank you for also having sleepovers with me. Thank you for listening to me and making me feel special regardless of my age. Thank you for letting me be your Velcro monkey and for running through the cow fields of England with me. You've inspired me more than you know.

Juliette, thank you for being my girl and for working through life's complicated moments with me. Thank you for being you and for staying up all night with me when I needed it most. And thank you for sifting through early copies of this manuscript and for being my sounding board for just about everything.

Grandma, Grandpa, Mama, and Papa, thank you for being the best grandparents I could have possibly imagined. You are all, to me, the most amazing examples of what incredible, long-lasting relationships look like and how to love your children regardless of who they love. You are all pioneers to me. I love you.

Kim Kelty, thank you for the push. Every single day.

Deb Jayne, thank you for believing in this manuscript and me. Without you I am not sure this manuscript would have ever seen a publisher's desk. I am forever grateful.

Lynzee, Kayla, and the entire Leo and Laine gang, thank you for understanding how important authenticity and gorgeous photos are for me, for taking the pressure of social media off my plate and for being a part of my team and most importantly my friends.

Michelle Mekky and the entire Mekky Media Relations Team, thank you for believing in my vision and taking my dream to new heights. And Bill, thank you for calling me back when you still had no idea what you were getting into. I am so very grateful. Thank you for welcoming me into the family so lovingly.

Camilla Michael, Christian Blonshine, Allison Janse, Lindsey Mach, and the entire team at HCI Books, I will never forget the moment I read the email from you, realizing I was going to be a published author. It was one of the most exciting moments of my life and it's only gotten more exciting since then. Thank you for believing in my story and in me and for welcoming me into the HCI family. I am honored to be working with you.

Susan Dickson, thank you for reminding me to ask empowering questions.

Laurie Chittenden and Polly Rosenwaike, thank you for your edits and for taking time to comb through all the details with me and making sure that I was able to produce the best possible version of my story to the world. Your time, care, and energy with my life story mean everything to me.

Auntie, I know you can't actually read this, but somehow I feel like you will. Thank you for being so selfless all those years ago and helping to create me. Thank you for your laugh, and your smile, and for always reminding me that you were my number one fan. The list of things I would give so I could hug you on earth one more time is long, but I feel your arms wrapped around me every day and know that it is your inspiration that gets me to keep going every time I want to stop doing anything in my life that will ultimately serve me. I will always love you.

ABOUT THE AUTHOR

Chelsea Austin Montgomery-Duban Wächter, otherwise known as Chelsea Austin, is a writer, speaker, and self-worth advocate from Malibu, California. Raised by two of the most incredible parents, her dads, Chelsea has taken her story of being raised by two gay men and used it as a platform to spread love and acceptance and has advocated for the LGBTQ+ community since she was in high school. In 2010, she was voted one of the Top Fifteen LGBT Activists in the Los Angeles area. In 2015, Chelsea graduated magna cum laude from Muhlenberg College with a degree in theater and dance.

After a successful, but ultimately unfulfilling career in real estate, Chelsea dropped everything to take control of her life's journey. Inspired by her own path Chelsea now spends her days as a nationally recognized writer, speaker, advocate, and certified professional coach on a mission to help others discover their self-worth. Whether it's through her blog, "The Girl with Five Names," her podcast,

"Worthiness Warriors," or speaking engagements, Chelsea believes in spreading positivity and bringing love and joy to as many individuals as possible.

Chelsea fuels her passion for the arts through her philanthropy. In 2020, Chelsea cofounded Dance in Color with her husband and close friends. Dance in Color is an organization that provides scholarships to young dancers of color in order for them to pursue their dreams through dance and ultimately create systemic change in the dance world.

Chelsea resides in Los Angeles with her amazing husband, Dominic, and their sweet puppy, Moe. To learn more visit chelseaaustin.com.

ARE YOU READY TO BE INEXPLICABLY YOU?

Chelsea is excited and ready to partner with you, your team, school, or organization to *Flip the Script* and build the life of your dreams. To book Chelsea for an event or workshop contact Wendy Kurtz at wkurtz@ElizabethCharles.com or call (407) 876-7730. For all media inquiries please email ChelseaAustinPR@mekkymedia. com.